D1570433

Paris Discovered

EXPLORATIONS IN THE CITY OF LIGHT

EXPLORATIONS IN THE CITY OF LIGHT

MARY McAULIFFE

ELYSIAN EDITIONS

PRINCETON BOOK COMPANY, PUBLISHERS

For Jack

The chapters in this book are based on articles that appeared in *Paris Notes*.

Jacket and text design by Melissa Farris and John McMenamin.
Drawings of Gertrude Stein and George Gershwin by John McMenamin.
Composition by Mulberry Tree Press, Inc.

All photographs, except where noted, are by Jack McAuliffe.

Library of Congress Cataloging-in-Publication Data

McAuliffe, Mary.
  Paris discovered: explorations in the city of light/Mary McAuliffe
        p.cm.
        Includes index.
    ISBN 0-87127-287-3
        1. Paris (France)—Description and travel.
    2. Paris (France)—History.

    DC707.M442 2006
    914.4/3610484 22

                          2006045245

Published by Elysian Editions™
An imprint of Princeton Book Company, Publishers
614 Route 130
Hightstown, NJ 08520
www.princetonbookcompany.com

6 5 4 3 2 1

Also from Elysian Editions:
The Magic of Provence and *Love in Provence*
both by Yvone Lenard

Contents

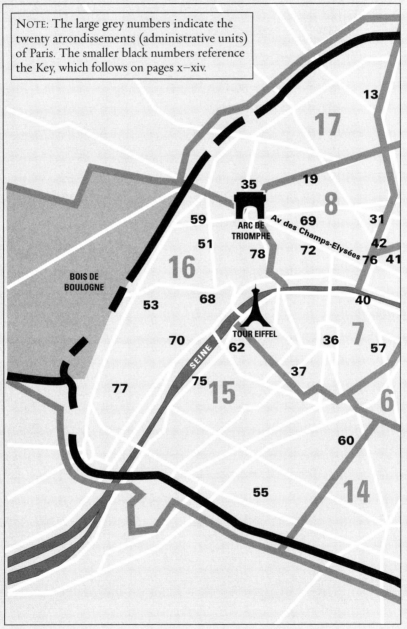

Map of Paris

NOTE: The large grey numbers indicate the
twenty arrondissements (administrative units)
of Paris. The smaller black numbers reference
the Key, which follows on pages x–xiv.

13

17

35

19

8

59

ARC DE
TRIOMPHE

69

Av des Champs-Elysées

31

51

78

72

42

76   41

16

BOIS DE
BOULOGNE

53

68

40

70

TOUR EIFFEL

SEINE

62

36

7

57

77

75

15

37

6

60

55

14

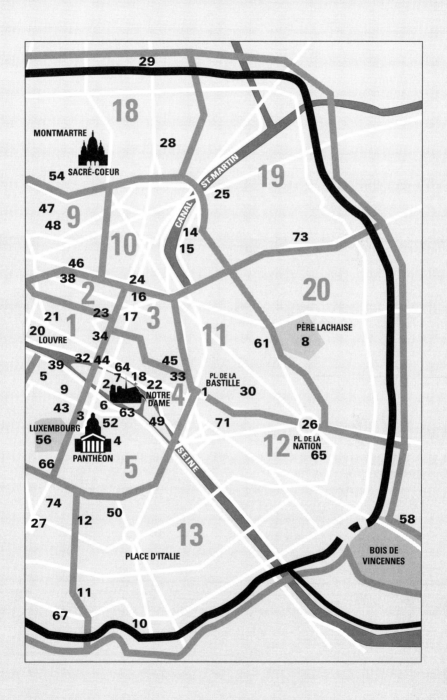

KEY TO SELECTED SITES IN

Paris Discovered

ALL SITES ARE IDENTIFIED BY ARRONDISSEMENT. SOME locations include more than one site, and some sites are referred to in more than one chapter. The chapter or chapters in which each of these sites is mentioned is included in italics at the end of each entry.

1. PLACE DE LA BASTILLE, at intersection of 4th, 11th and 12th arrondissements
   - ⚜ Picture of ELEPHANT OF THE BASTILLE, in the Rue de Lyon exit from the No. 1 line, Bastille Métro station (*Preface*)
   - ⚜ Vestiges of the BASTILLE in the Bastille station of the No. 5 Métro line (*Walls of Paris*)
   - ⚜ Adjacent MARINA OF THE PARIS ARSENAL (*Enchanted Canal*)

2. NOTRE-DAME, Ile de la Cité, 4th (*Notre-Dame, Headless Saint, Little Giant, Victor Hugo's Legacy*)
   - ⚜ CRYPTE ARCHÉOLOGIQUE, Place du Parvis-Notre-Dame, 4th (*Notre-Dame, Paris Y1K, Walls of Paris*)
   - ⚜ MUSÉE DE NOTRE-DAME DE PARIS, 10 Rue du Cloître-Notre-Dame, 4th (*Little Giant*)

3. MUSÉE NATIONAL DU MOYEN AGE, THERMES AND HÔTEL DE CLUNY, 6 Place Paul-Painlevé, 5th (*Notre-Dame, Paris Y1K*)

4. GALLO-ROMAN ARENA (ARÈNES DE LUTÈCE), Rue Monge at Rue de Navarre, 5th (*Paris Y1K*)
   - ⚜ L'ARCHE DE LA BIÈVRE, beneath post office at 30 Rue du Cardinal-Lemoine (at the corner of Rue des Ecoles), 5th (*Lost River, Walls of Paris*)
   - ⚜ SECTION OF TWELFTH-CENTURY WALL, Rue Clovis at Rue du Cardinal-Lemoine, 5th (*Walls of Paris*)

5. SAINT-GERMAIN-DES-PRÉS, 3 Place St-Germain-des-Prés, 6th (*Paris Y1K, Pathways to the Past*)
   - ⚜ HÔTEL D'YORK, 56 Rue Jacob, 6th (*Founding Fathers*)

6. SAINT-JULIEN-LE-PAUVRE, 1 Rue Saint-Julien-le-Pauvre, 5th (*Paris Y1K, Pathways to the Past*)
   - ⚜ RUE DE LA BÛCHERIE, RUE DE BIÈVRE, RUE DES GRANDS-DEGRÉS, and RUE GALANDE, 5th (*Pathways to the Past, Lost River*)

7. 9-11 QUAI AUX FLEURS (4th), site of Héloïse's residence and love affair with Abélard (*Abélard and Héloïse*)
   ⚜ SAINT-AIGNAN, 19 Rue des Ursins, 4th (*Hidden Chapel*)

8. PÈRE-LACHAISE CEMETERY, 20th (*Abélard and Héloïse, The Divine Miss B, Prelude to Chopin, The Few and the Daring*)

9. COUR DE ROHAN, 6th (*Pathways to the Past*)
   ⚜ COUR DU COMMERCE SAINT-ANDRÉ, 6th (*Pathways to the Past, Walls of Paris*) (4 Cour du Commerce Saint-André includes a three-story tower from Paris' twelfth-century wall)
   ⚜ CAFÉ PROCOPE, 13 Rue de l'Ancienne-Comédie, 6th (*Founding Fathers*)

10. PARC KELLERMANN, Boulevard Kellermann, 13th (*Lost River*)

11. CITÉ FLORALE, 13th, between Place de Rungis and Parc Montsouris (*Lost River, Flower Bowers*)

12. CITÉ FLEURIE, 65 Boulevard Arago, 13th (*Flower Bowers*)

13. CITÉ DES FLEURS, between Avenue de Clichy and Rue de La Jonquière, 17th (*Flower Bowers*)

14. CANAL SAINT-MARTIN, 19th, 10th and 11th (*Enchanted Canal*)

15. HÔPITAL SAINT-LOUIS, 2 Place du Docteur-Alfred-Fournier, on Rue Bichat, 10th (*Enchanted Canal, Henri le Grand*)

16. FORMER ABBEY CHURCH OF SAINT-MARTIN-DES-CHAMPS (now part of the Musée des Arts et Métiers), 292 Rue Saint-Martin, entrance at 60 Rue Réaumur, 3rd (*Oldest House in Paris, Statues of Liberty*)

17. HOUSE OF NICOLAS FLAMEL, 51 Rue de Montmorency, 3rd (*Oldest House in Paris*)

18. 11 AND 13 RUE FRANÇOIS-MIRON, 4th (*Oldest House in Paris*)

19. PARC MONCEAU, Boulevard de Courcelles, 8th (*Beaumont Boys, Walls of Paris, Statues of Liberty*)
   ⚜ The ROTONDE DE CHARTRES, the small rotunda that once was the Monceau tollhouse, is located at the park's Boulevard de Courcelles entrance (*Walls of Paris*).

20. LOUVRE, 1st (*Walls of Paris, Henri le Grand, Little Giant, Great Art Heist*)
   ⚜ ARC DE TRIOMPHE DU CARROUSEL, Place du Carrousel, 1st (*Little Giant*)

21. COMÉDIE-FRANÇAISE, Place André-Malraux, 1st (*The Divine Miss B, Victor Hugo's Legacy*)
   ⚜ PLAQUE AND BAS-RELIEF OF JEANNE D'ARC'S HEAD, marking the site of the fortified Saint-Honoré gate in the original fourteenth-century Paris walls. At 161-163 Rue Saint-Honoré at Place André-Malraux, between the Louvre and the Palais Royal, 1st (*Walls of Paris, Maid of Orléans*)
   ⚜ FRÉMIET'S HEROIC GOLDEN STATUE OF JEANNE D'ARC is nearby, in the Place des Pyramides, 1st

22. HÔTEL DE SENS, 1 Rue du Figuier, 4th (*A Difficult Queen*)
   ⚜ VILLAGE SAINT-PAUL, between Rue Saint-Paul, Rue de l'Ave Maria, Rue Charlemagne, and Rue des Jardins-Saint-Paul, 4th (*Village Saint-Paul*)

⚜ Institut de France and Académie Française, 6ᵀᴴ (*Little Giant, Victor Hugo's Legacy*)

40. Palace of the Legion of Honor (Hôtel de Salm), 2 Rue de Bellechasse, 7ᵗʰ (*Little Giant, Founding Fathers*)

⚜ National Assembly (Palais Bourbon), 33 Quai d'Orsay, 7ᵗʰ (*Little Giant*)

41. Place Vendôme, 1ˢᵗ (*Little Giant, Prelude to Chopin*)

42. Church of the Madeleine (Sainte-Marie-Madeleine), Place de la Madeleine, 8ᵗʰ (*Little Giant, Prelude to Chopin*)

43. Théâtre de l'Odéon, Place de l'Odéon, 6ᵗʰ (*The Divine Miss B*)

⚜ Sylvia Beach's Shakespeare and Company, 12 Rue de l'Odéon, 6ᵗʰ (*Gertrude Stein, American in Paris*)

44. Place du Châtelet, 1ˢᵗ and 4ᵗʰ

⚜ Théâtre Sarah Bernhardt (now the Théâtre de la Ville), 2 Place du Châtelet, 4ᵗʰ (*The Divine Miss B*)

⚜ Fountain, Place du Châtelet (*Little Giant*)

45. Musée Carnavalet, 23 Rue de Sévigné, 3ʳᵈ (*Mucha's Maidens, Down a Hidden Staircase*)

46. Passage des Panoramas (2ⁿᵈ), Passage Jouffroy (9ᵗʰ) and Passage Verdeau (9ᵗʰ), extending back on both sides from Boulevard Montmartre (*Prelude to Chopin*)

47. Musée de la Vie Romantique, 16 Rue Chaptal, 9ᵗʰ (*Prelude to Chopin*)

48. Square d'Orléans, Rue Taitbout at Rue Saint-Lazare, 9ᵗʰ (*Prelude to Chopin*)

49. Musée Adam-Mickiewicz, 6 Quai d'Orléans, on the Ile Saint-Louis, 4ᵗʰ (*Prelude to Chopin*)

50. Square René-le-Gall, 13ᵗʰ (*Victor Hugo's Legacy, Lost River*, and *The Few and the Daring*)

⚜ 41 Rue de Croulebarbe, formerly a tavern and a Victor Hugo haunt

⚜ Hôtel de la Reine-Blanche, 17 and 19 Rue des Gobelins, 13ᵗʰ (*Lost River*)

51. 124 Avenue Victor Hugo, 16ᵗʰ (Victor Hugo's last address)

52. Panthéon, Place du Panthéon, 5ᵗʰ (Victor Hugo and Jean Moulin are both buried here) (*Victor Hugo's Legacy, The Few and the Daring*)

53. Musée Marmottan-Monet, 2 Rue Louis-Boilly, 16ᵗʰ (*Forgotten Impressionist, Great Art Heist*)

54. Bateau-Lavoir, 13 Place Emile-Goudeau, 18ᵗʰ (*Laundry Boat to Beehive*)

55. La Ruche, Passage de Dantzig, 15ᵗʰ (*Laundry Boat to Beehive*)

56. Luxembourg Gardens, 6ᵗʰ (*Gertrude Stein, Statues of Liberty*)

⚜ Gertrude Stein's residence, 27 Rue de Fleurus, 6ᵗʰ (*Gertrude Stein*)

57. Musée Maillol, 61 Rue de Grenelle, 7ᵗʰ (*Sculptor's Muse*)

58. Château de Vincennes, Bois de Vincennes (*The Few and the Daring*)

59. 82-84 Avenue Foch, 16ᵗʰ (*The Few and the Daring*)

Preface

IN MANY WAYS, I OWE MY DISCOVERY OF PARIS—THE Paris of bricks and stone and accumulated centuries—to the Elephant of the Bastille. I had just attended a performance of the new musical, *Les Misérables*, in its 1986 pre-Broadway run, and a friend wanted to know what I thought of the elephant.

"What elephant?" I asked.

"Well, that's exactly the point," she retorted. "There wasn't one."

"Should there have been?"

She gave me a thoughtful look. "Haven't you read the book?"

"No," I had to admit. "But I intend to."

"Do," she said. "And then you'll see what I mean about the elephant."

Well, time passed, and I didn't read the book. After all, it's a big one, and in any case, I had read portions in high school and was familiar with the story. Why tackle any more of Victor Hugo's over-the-top prose? So when my husband's connection to the show brought me back to the theater for a second viewing, I simply looked more closely when Jean Valjean and little Cosette finally enter Paris. Where could an elephant possibly belong in this amazing—but completely urban—setting?

And then I saw it. It was small, but it was indeed an elephant, perched on top of a towering pile that dramatically evoked the slums of early nineteenth-century Paris. "Aha!" I thought, pleased to be able to report back to my friend that this Broadway-bound production had not ignored her favorite pachyderm after all.

"But it was barely visible," she scoffed. "Just this little thing perched up there, like a lamp or something."

Abashed, I changed the subject and didn't think of it again until, on a subsequent trip to Paris, I found myself exiting the Métro at the Bastille stop. "Look!" I called to my husband, as I came to a complete halt.

"What is it?" he asked, fighting his way back against pedestrian traffic to reach my side.

"There," I said, pointing to a picture on the wall, where the City of Paris had placed one of a number of obviously historical prints. Such uplifting decor was not in itself unusual. Not only has the City sprayed its many Métro stations with a special perfume, and auditioned hundreds of musicians for the right to busk along its labyrinthine subway corridors, but it has individually decorated each of its downtown stations. This meant a surprisingly cheerful mural of July 14's bloody events for the Bastille stop, including an unexpected pair of Dame Edna-style spectacles on one of the participants.

But the picture that grabbed my attention had nothing to do with the fall of the Bastille. It was a drawing of an elephant—obviously huge, and just as obviously a part of an urban setting.

"Do you suppose there really *was* an elephant here once?" I asked my husband. "Right here, at the Place de la Bastille?"

"Haven't you read the book yet?" he asked.

There it was again. That overgrown book. Still, an idea had taken hold, and on looking back, I now realize that this moment marked the beginning of my search—a search for Paris.

I am an historian by training and trade as well as by general inclination. That inclination, however I may try to disguise it, amounts to a passion. Whenever I encounter something that catches my attention, I invariably want to find out where it came from, who and what it has affected, and how it has gone about doing whatever it has done.

To use the word that was popular a few years back, I may be looking for "roots," but I think it's far more than that. Genealogy, of and by itself, does not interest me. Things that are old do not automatically intrigue me. Contrary to stereotype, I am not a packrat; quite the opposite, in fact. I have seen too much stuff over the course of my life that has been collected for far too long.

And yet I have a real weakness for certain persons, places, and things that offer tangible links with the past. The French have a word for it—*patrimoine.* But they infuse the word with far more vitality and passion than our English "patrimony," which comes across as pretty thin soup by comparison. Even "heritage" doesn't really do it. Yes, there's a certain amount of chest-thumping nationalism in *patrimoine*, but there is an even stronger sense that the past has real value, to be relished and cherished right up there with the finer things of life.

Perhaps two thousand years of history will do that to you, but even a few decades will do, if the subject is sufficiently compelling. I recall a small hand-lettered notice in the Musée Jean-Moulin, Paris' museum of the Resistance. Scrawled in black, it reads (in part, and in translation): "Down with the traitors of Vichy! Down with the Collaboration! Long live General de Gaulle, the savior of France and of our liberty!...Resist!" The entire museum, which is small, is filled with attention-riveting items, but this one spoke so directly across the years that it moved me to tears.

Perhaps it's not such a long leap, after all, from Hugo's valiant but doomed band of revolutionaries in *Les Misérables* to the equally valiant and doomed members of Paris' Resistance to the Nazi Occupation.

———

Yes, I did read *Les Misérables* in its entirety, and I found the elephant—a full-scale plaster and wood model for a forgotten Napoleonic monument, left to molder for several decades on the Place de la Bastille. I found the elephant about two-thirds of the way through the book, when Gavroche climbs into his hideout in the rotting plaster carcass. True to form, Hugo manages to romanticize the poor beast, tell how it got there, and portray the social evils that surround it, all in several dense pages. It's terrific stuff.

But I also discovered something else. Hugo knew his Paris, with its open sewers and darkened slums. He had walked its streets and knew the hunger, the filth, and the despair. He was an onlooker of the uprising of 1832 that he writes about, and the death of a small boy carrying a Tricolor may have provided the inspiration for little Gavroche.

Many streets have entirely vanished since Hugo's day, and many others have changed names. In the 1850s and 1860s, Baron Georges Haussmann, Napoléon III's formidable city planner, leveled much of medieval Paris, whose winding alleys had over the centuries become fetid slums, fostering uprisings of the sort that Hugo so movingly depicts. Haussmann may have wanted a cleaner and more modern Paris, but he also wanted to suppress social and political turmoil. Wider streets meant fewer pockets where barricades like the one at the Corinth tavern could rise. Wider streets made it easier for the military to march.

In fact, Hugo wrote *Les Misérables* as a kind of memory piece, written in exile on the isles of Jersey and Guernsey, where he fled at the outset of Napoléon III's imperial rule. By this time, Hugo had become an outspoken critic of the kind of society that could so devastatingly penalize someone like Jean Valjean simply for stealing a loaf of bread.

This is not the place to analyze Hugo's politics, which were not as simple as he would have liked them to appear. He was, after all, a complex man. Still, he had been there and seen it. He knew his Paris. And he knew that in demolishing those narrow streets, Haussmann had not diminished poverty—only the means to resist.

———

What follows is a collection of essays based on articles that I have written over the past five years for *Paris Notes*, a valuable monthly publication for anyone who enjoys learning new ways to experience this extraordinary city. Each of my essays is the result of a personal exploration, the outcome of a small prick of curiosity or of a larger and more burning desire to discover and better understand some aspect of the City of Light. In each case, I have embarked on a journey of discovery, and invariably I've been surprised by the riches I have found.

I have learned to look for patterns, even where most unlikely, and to sleuth out forgotten bits of Paris' past. In the process, I have often found one discovery leading to another, sometimes in completely unexpected ways. Who would have guessed, for example, that the lovely and virtually unknown park, Square René-le-Gall, would have led me in so many topical directions, or that the stunning courtyard of the Hôpital Saint-Louis would have given me insight into the medieval aqueducts of Paris as well as into its founder, the ever-astonishing Henri IV?

As my collection of articles and discoveries grew, it seemed natural to draw them together. The result is this book, which proceeds in a roughly chronological fashion. Although the reader may wish to dip randomly into the collection, he or she may find it more rewarding to proceed in order, discovering how each subject fits into an ever-richer and organic whole.

My own journey of discovery has been immeasurably enriched by the assistance and encouragement of a number of special people along the way. In particular, I would like to thank Mark Eversman, publisher and editor of *Paris Notes,* for his encouragement and guidance. A writer could not hope for a more supportive editor, and I am grateful to him for allowing me to explore the paths I've taken.

I would also like to thank the many gracious Parisians who have assisted me, sharing their particular historical passions and giving me access to places I might not otherwise have had the opportunity to see. In particular, I would like to thank the Mairie de Paris (City Hall), and especially Francis Jestin, who assisted me on several occasions. My thanks as well to Soeur Jacqueline Louineau, of the Sacrés-Coeurs de Jésus et Marie, who proved a true angel of mercy on one especially absorbing quest. I am also deeply indebted to Gérard Duserre, Jean-Luc Largier and Gilles Thomas, who have enthusiastically answered reams of questions about the medieval labyrinths that lurk beneath Paris' surface, and have taken mc and my husband to places where—they assure me— no American has ever gone before.

A special thanks to my daughter, Mavyn, who has staunchly read almost every one of these essays in draft form, contributing her perceptive criticism as well as her unfailing encouragement and support. Many thanks as well to my son-in-law, Jay, who provided insightful advice, including a major assist on the title.

And last, my enduring thanks and love to my husband, Jack, who has shared every step of these adventures with me, pounding miles of Paris pavement, taking the wonderful pictures that accompany these articles, and serving in every capacity from literary agent to transportation guru. Paris is unquestionably a city for lovers, and it has been a privilege and a delight to discover so many of its wonders by his side.

NOTE

PARIS IS DIVIDED INTO TWENTY ARRONDISSEMENTS, or administrative units, each having its own *mairie*, or city hall. City hall for all of Paris is the Mairie de Paris, located in the Hôtel de Ville.

The first twelve arrondissements, spiraling outward from the center of Paris, date from 1795. The remaining eight were added in 1860, completing the arrondissements and establishing Paris' administrative limits as they exist today.

The Bois de Boulogne and the Bois de Vincennes, at the far edges of Paris, belong to the city but lie outside of these arrondissements.

Please note that throughout the text, arrondissement locations are indicated by their numbers ("12th" for 12th arrondissement).

I

A CATHEDRAL for the AGES

I.

Notre-Dame

STAND IN THE PLACE DU PARVIS FACING THE GREAT Cathedral of Notre-Dame, and you will be gazing at a direct link with the twelfth century. Stand close, for originally that was how Notre-Dame was meant to be seen. Before Baron Haussmann flattened an entire neighborhood to create a far vaster cathedral square, or even before Notre-Dame acquired its famed flying buttresses, the people of Paris approached their cathedral through narrow byways, catching glimpses of a portal here or a tower there, until at last they stood before the Western façade and looked up. And up and up. For this was a cathedral built to be seen and appreciated from below, not from afar.

Come closer, and you will begin to understand the impact of those three intricately carved portals, topped by the stately Gallery of Kings, magnificent rose window, lacy colonnade, and mammoth towers. From the farthest reaches of Notre-Dame's Place du Parvis, these very same components somehow seem less stirring. But come close, and Notre-Dame exerts the full impact of its grandeur and power.

You will also be standing on history, for beneath your feet lie the remains of the ancient cathedral that preceded Notre-

Dame. Excavations for an underground parking garage uncovered a dense patchwork of archeological ruins going back to Gallo-Roman times, including bits and pieces of old cathedral foundations. Long buried beneath the rubble of the centuries, these dusty bricks and stones (which you can visit in the nearby Crypte Archéologique) help to tell the complex story of this tip of the Ile de la Cité, and of Notre-Dame's early years.

Parisians have been piecing together this story ever since the early 1700s, when workmen digging a burial vault beneath Notre-Dame's chancel were startled to encounter the remains of a first-century Gallo-Roman shrine dedicated to Jupiter. This so-called Pilier des Nautes (or Boatmen's Pillar), which you can visit in the Musée du Moyen Age (6 Place Paul-Painlevé, 5th), is quite likely the oldest surviving sculpture in Paris—providing proof that Parisians have worshiped at the eastern end of the Ile de la Cité since earliest times.

After Christianity replaced the Roman gods, Parisians consecrated this end of the island to Christian worship, constructing the impressive cathedral whose foundations—outlined on the Place du Parvis—lie beneath your feet. This cathedral, discovered in 1847 during major renovations on Notre-Dame's façade, dates from the remote sixth century, and possibly even earlier. Majestically proportioned, it stretched some 118 feet wide by 230 feet long—although its exact length will forever remain a question, as this early cathedral's eastern end completely disappeared during Notre-Dame's construction. Dedicated to Saint-Etienne, or Saint Stephen, this extraordinary structure gloried in decorations of marble and mosaic, whose remnants (along with fragments of Notre-Dame's original sculpture) you can find in the Musée du Moyen Age.

A certain haze descends over what happened next, during those dark and dangerous years before Notre-Dame de Paris rose on this end of the island, replacing the ancient cathedral. Older versions of the story speak of a small chapel dedicated to Notre-Dame that was destroyed by Vikings and then replaced by a larger edifice. This in turn was dismantled—along with the decaying cathedral of Saint-Etienne—when Maurice de Sully began to send the current Notre-Dame skyward. But more recent research proposes that the increasingly popular Virgin simply encroached on Saint-Etienne. For a time, the old cathedral was dedicated to both. And then sometime around the late tenth century, the Blessed Virgin became the sole dedicatee. Same building, in other words, but a different name.

If this is what actually happened, then the extensive repairs carried out on the Church of the Blessed Mary during the second quarter of the twelfth century actually spruced up the ancient cathedral, which would have been in reasonably good shape when Sully became Bishop of Paris in 1160. But spruced up or not, the ancient edifice was definitely out of date, especially compared with the stunning renovations that Abbot Suger had recently carried out on the nearby abbey church of Saint-Denis. Bishops throughout France were in a building mode by the middle years of the twelfth century, and Sully was not to be outdone. He would erect a splendid new edifice for the Blessed Virgin, and he would build for the ages.

Sully, a man of humble origins who had begged for food during his student years in Paris, was a dynamo with vision. An organizational genius, he quickly realized that to construct a new cathedral in the already-dense urban fabric of the Ile de la Cité would require a major effort in what we today would call urban planning. Not only did he plan, build, and finance an enormous and pathbreaking cathedral within his own lifetime, but also he altered the entire cityscape on this end of the island, erecting and demolishing buildings with tornado force.

By the time of his death in 1196, Sully had leveled the old Bishop's Palace and Hôtel-Dieu (charity hospice) and rebuilt them in far grander style to the south of his new cathedral—on land that was so marshy that foundations had to plunge thirty feet below the surface for secure footing. To provide sufficient land for the new cathedral's choir and apse, he used landfill to extend the Ile de la Cité eastward, joining it with a small island just offshore. And then, with remarkable persistence, he negotiated his way through a welter of irate property-holders to pierce a new street, with the then-unheard-of width of twenty feet, right to Notre-Dame's front door. (You can see the outlines of this street, the Rue Neuve Notre-Dame, on the Place du Parvis).

No less a personage than the Pope is credited with laying the cornerstone for Sully's vast cathedral in 1163. Hundreds of workers now descended on the site, which began to rise on the marshy land to the east of the old edifice and the decaying Gallo-Roman wall. Here stonecutters, masons, carpenters, blacksmiths, hodmen, water carriers, lime workers, and cart drivers all converged, along with a steady stream of bargemen, who unloaded massive blocks of stone—extracted from quarries south of town—at a nearby quay. Despite the obvious challenge of constructing on marshy soil, the building proceeded quickly and without incident, with Sully maintaining a remarkable degree of order throughout.

We do not know the name of the first architect who under-took this mammoth project, but we do know that by 1177—after less than fifteen years—the eastern end of Notre-Dame was virtually complete, all the way to its massive transepts. Only the work of vaulting the highest reaches remained. By May 19, 1182, when a papal legate consecrated the new high altar, the cathe-dral's entire eastern portion was finished.

Sully was blessed with a long life, and by the time he died, much of his cathedral's western portion, or nave, was also com-plete. Next came the cathedral front, or façade, which rose steadily upward until 1245, when those in charge decided to leave the towers as they were, without steeples—opting instead for a major spire above the cathedral crossing.

During this time, the eastern portions of the old cathedral must have been razed, to make way for the western march of the new. This made room not only for the new cathedral but also for the cathedral square, the *parvis*, that Sully had envisioned all those years before.

If, one fine day in 1220 (at the age of twenty), you had stood shifting about in your long tunic and cloak in this small *parvis*, gazing upward at Notre-Dame, you would have seen that the façade had proceeded as far as the Gallery of Kings, with its twenty-eight dramatically colored statues, and already included those three famous portals, or doorways. Of these, the one on the right appears to you to be more weathered than the others. Hardly surprising, as it was created for the old cathedral, and then moved to its new site after rededication to the Virgin's mother, Saint Anne. You are particularly awed by the depiction of Christ of the Second Coming in the central portal, The Last Judgment. But your favorite is the portal on the left, The Coronation of the Virgin, and you have fine taste, indeed. You probably care little that future generations will declare this the cathedral's masterpiece. You only know that you like its friendly-looking angels, its depictions of local saints (St. Geneviève and a headless St. Denis), as well as those small reliefs along the doorposts that are devoted to the everyday life you know so well. You could not possibly imagine that these small depictions of medieval life will be among the few of Notre-Dame's original sculptures to make it intact to the twenty-first century.

You would also be amazed to learn that the cathedral you are so intently admiring will have quite a different look within only a very few years. Despite the obvious grandeur of Sully's original vision—an edifice stretching 402 feet long, 131 feet wide, and a daring 108 feet upward to its topmost vaulting—his cathedral turned out to be surprisingly dark inside. What to do?

After much head-scratching, Sully's successors decided on an audacious renovation. They lengthened the topmost (clerestory) windows, thereby eliminating the row of small round pierced windows, or oculi, that opened onto eaves above the tribune vaults (there's a nineteenth-century approximation of the original arrangement along the transept). What that meant was a thorough rebuilding, bringing the cathedral from four elevations to three, and replacing the sloping side roofs with flat ones. But this now introduced another problem, for the resulting flat roof surface did not drain properly. The solution—an innovation that is still in use today—included the introduction of flying buttresses.

Flying buttresses? You mean, they weren't there to begin with? Well, no. Or—more accurately—probably not. There were buttresses of course, right from the outset, but not those famous flying ones. These arrived sometime around the 1220s, while the façade was still rising, and were essentially an elaborate form of gutter—channeled along the top to carry floods of roof water downward and outward to those captivating stone gargoyles, which spouted it well beyond the building.

How unromantic! Didn't the flying buttresses at least serve some sort of structural purpose—especially after those clerestory windows were lengthened? Probably not. Despite a lot of earlier conjecture to the contrary, the latest word on the subject (Alain Erlande-Brandenburg's *Notre-Dame de Paris*) is that Notre-Dame's flying buttresses were structurally too weak to do much in the way of countering the stone vaulting's outward thrust. If you doubt this, take another look at these buttresses' extreme thinness and length, not to mention the audacious piercing through their headstones. No, unlike other cathedrals, Notre-Dame's flying buttresses were—and remain—primarily gutters. And extremely successful ones, at that.

Returning to the cathedral *parvis* in 1250 (you have by now achieved the advanced medieval age of fifty), you note the huge changes made to the building since you were last here. These include those flying buttresses and that major alteration to windows and roofline, as well as completion of the façade, topped by two enormous towers. But your gaze is quite properly fixed on the façade's enormous rose window— an extraordinary achievement, breathtakingly free of supporting stonework, despite its size.

A return visit in the 1270s (you obviously are a tough sort) reveals even more change. Construction has proceeded rapidly on a series of small chapels between the flying buttresses—an unattractive development, in your opinion (and that of many others). To prevent the cathedral exterior from looking over-stuffed, major renovations have also begun on both transepts, to extend them beyond the chapel walls. To your delight, this latest renovation has brought the addition of two huge rose windows—the one to the south quite possibly by the same architect who created nearby Sainte-Chapelle.

Fortunately you are not able to make another visit several centuries later, following the Revolution. Despite a fairly recent updating of chancel and choir, any bystander of the early 1800s would soon note Notre-Dame's woebegone appearance, its aging structure dismal, dark, and sadly neglected. Revolutionary mobs have done the most serious damage, making off with or destroying anything within reach, but there have also been destructive acts of a more calculated sort—most notably the mutilation of the cathedral's grand central portal, hacked apart to allow easier passage of processionals. Mobs have attacked the Bishop's Palace as well, leading to its demolition.

Enter Victor Hugo, whose 1831 novel, *Notre-Dame de Paris* (or *The Hunchback of Notre-Dame*), made a cause célèbre of the dying cathedral. Responding to popular demand, the government now agreed to underwrite a huge restoration program, and Jean-Baptiste Lassus and Eugène Viollet-le-Duc bravely undertook the work (Lassus died early on, leaving Viollet-le-Duc to carry on alone). The outcome, the result of almost two decades of meticulous research and inevitable guesswork, is the Notre-Dame that you see today.

Is this the Notre-Dame of the thirteenth century? Not

exactly, although significant portions are as close as careful research can make them. Aiding the effort, fragments of the cathedral's original sculpture began to turn up during the project's early stages, providing essential references for restoration. As for the rest, Viollet-le-Duc's imagination filled in the gaps. Fortunately for us, even his more fanciful creations here are a triumph—notably those famous gargoyles and chimeras, as well as his spire, whose original had long since disappeared.

Notre-Dame's neighborhood has of course vastly improved since Victor Hugo's day, although Bishop Sully certainly would not recognize Baron Haussmann's vastly expanded *parvis.* Still, if you can catch a glimpse of Notre-Dame's spire from the ancient Rue des Chantres or Place Maubert, and then follow the narrowest lanes you can find to the great cathedral's western portals, you will be treading the path that countless medieval students and clerics have taken before you.

And then look up, and up, relishing this direct link with a distant past. Here is Notre-Dame, the noble survivor of the centuries. Here is Notre-Dame—truly a cathedral for the ages.

II

TIME TRAVELING

2.

Paris Y1K

YOU HAVE NOW DIPPED BACK EIGHT CENTURIES INTO Paris' past, when Notre-Dame was rising skyward and the city was well on its way to glory. But don't forget what a difference a couple of centuries can make. Twelfth-century Paris may have been a center of energy and light, but only two centuries before, at the turn of the first millennium, it wasn't at all clear that Paris was even going to survive.

Abandoned by the Romans and struggling to recover from the Vikings, Paris by the first millennium had shrunk to scarcely more than the walled Cité, a marshy waystation along the decaying roadway linking Rome to the Channel. Its inhabitants, who subsisted on a diet that would have shocked Michelin, slogged through their dreary days without benefit of *haute couture* or sidewalk cafés, keeping their heads down to avoid trouble. Law and order was an endangered species, and violence a fact of life. Word had already spread that Fulk the Black, the volcanic count of neighboring Anjou, had reacted to a wifely indiscretion by burning his spouse at the stake. Others were equally edgy. It would not have taken much to convince any of Paris' hard-pressed residents that the end of the world was about to come. Indeed, from any reasonable standpoint, it already had.

Yet somehow these hard-pressed Parisians managed to hang on, building on foundations that stretched back over one thousand years. With some determination and imagination, you can revisit some of those foundations, recreating the Paris that so stubbornly held its ground a millennium ago.

First, note the site—a hill-ringed basin lying at the Seine's confluence with the Oise and the Marne. Sometime around 250 BC, the Parisii Celts invaded the region and set up housekeeping on the largest of the Seine's islands (now the Ile de la Cité), ignoring their damp basements in the happy expectation that their fortified island would at least be safe. Fishermen and boatmen, they prospered in this watery locale.

But eventually the Romans took notice, relentlessly pushing in and occupying the town (which they called Lutetia) in 52 BC. By the first century AD, they had rebuilt the bridges and erected a temple and administrative buildings on the Ile de la Cité. Avoiding the flood-prone island and the soggy marshes of the Seine's banks for anything other than 9-to-5 pursuits, they set up living quarters in their usual style on the Left Bank hill (now Montagne Sainte-Geneviève) to the south. Here they created a small metropolis, with a forum between what now are the Luxembourg Gardens and the Panthéon, public baths (one of which can still be seen adjoining the Hôtel de Cluny, 5th), and an amphitheater (Rue Monge at Rue de Navarre, 5th). In addition, they built an aqueduct leading in from the south, paralleling what now is Rue Saint-Jacques. Remains of a small theater have also been found beneath the Lycée Saint-Louis, 6th.

Lutetia's role as a strategic crossroads grew, with its bridges (now the Petit Pont and Pont Notre-Dame) linking what became Rue Saint-Martin on the Right Bank with Rue Saint-Jacques on the Left. By the second century AD, it contained a population of around 10,000—considerably less than the 80,000 of Lyons or the 1,000,000 of Rome itself, but not bad, all things considered.

Barbarians on the march attacked the Left Bank settlement several times in the third and fourth centuries, prompting its beleaguered inhabitants to construct walls around the Cité and forum, and to turn the entire town into a military outpost. At about the same time, the arrival of St. Denis, the town's first bishop, added a new element to the mix. Although St. Denis' mission to Lutetia ended in martyrdom, he succeeded in creating a foothold for Christianity. And from this point on, as the Empire crumbled and Roman influence waned, Christianity played an ever-growing role in keeping the town that now was called Paris (after the Celtic Parisii) from going under. In 451 AD, when Attila the Hun prepared to sack the place, a saintly young woman named Geneviève urged the terrified Parisians to pray for deliverance. Attila turned aside—opting instead for Orléans—and Geneviève (who on another occasion saved the city from starvation) eventually became the city's patron saint.

By the sixth century, following the conversion of Clovis I, King of the Franks, ancestors of some of Paris' most famous churches and abbeys were beginning to appear. Following the Roman precedent of establishing official buildings at the western end of the Cité and religious structures to the east, Parisian Christians erected a cathedral group of several churches at the eastern end of the island, including the cathedral of Saint-Etienne. Clovis, who made Paris his capital, made a significant addition to this ecclesiastical presence by building an impressive abbey church on the Left Bank later known as Sainte-Geneviève. Not many years after, Clovis' son, Childebert, founded the monastery that became known as Saint-Germain-des-Prés (after Saint Germain, bishop of Paris). Members of the royal family had their final resting place here from Childebert on, until Dagobert changed the royal burial site to the abbey of Saint-Denis.

During the years that followed, other important Paris churches and abbeys had their start, including Saint-Marcel and Saint-Martin-des-Champs. A forebear of little Saint-Julien-le-Pauvre emerged in the sixth century, while predecessors of Saint-Germain-l'Auxerrois, Saint-Gervais-Saint-Protais, and Saint-Merri appeared soon after. Adding to Paris' importance as a trade center, King Dagobert I established the famous Lendit fair to the north of town, under the auspices of the growing abbey of Saint-Denis. Until the early years of the ninth century, Paris managed in a modest way to prosper.

Prosperity, however modest, proved its undoing, for now the dreaded sails of the Viking dragon ships appeared, striking terror as they came. The entire population of Paris retreated to the walled Cité for a full year in 885–86, as its men fought the Viking besiegers. At length, the Vikings headed upstream into Burgundy. A century of political disruption and chaos followed.

By the first millennium, Paris still was reeling from this knockout blow. Shrunken to scarcely more than the walled Cité, the town had become a pitiful tangle of marsh and weeds. Everywhere, townsfolk could see forlorn reminders of an ancient and far grander past—whether the Roman walls encasing the Cité, or the mysterious remains of amphitheater and baths, or the great churches and abbeys with their huddles of dependent villages along the Seine's shores. Recovery would begin in the following century, under the new Capetian monarchs, and within another century after that, the city would gradually grow to encompass these ecclesiastical bastions, slowly spreading to the right and left banks of the Seine.

But the brave and undoubtedly discouraged Parisians of the year 1000 did not know this. When, in an act of consummate faith, they began to erect the western tower of Saint-Germain-des-Prés, they had no reassurance that either it or they would make it to the following year. Little did they know that this rugged First Millennium tower would still be standing guard over its quarter of Paris one thousand years later, quietly withstanding the tides of history, and dramatically linking that distant age to our own.

3.

Abélard and Héloïse

OF COURSE, IT WAS A SCANDAL. BUT WHEN ABÉLARD and Héloïse began their love affair in Paris, sometime around the year 1118, they could hardly have guessed that people would still be talking about them nine centuries later.

Admittedly, Peter Abélard was the sort who attracted gossip. Arrogant and attractive, he had given up a knighthood in Brittany for a scholar's life in Paris, delighting in intellectual combat, in which he excelled. After repeated clashes with those he deemed his intellectual inferiors, he at last landed the job of his dreams, teaching at the cathedral school of Notre-Dame. Students flocked from all over Europe, bringing him wealth and fame.

And then, at the pinnacle of success, his gaze fell on Héloïse. Young and pious (the niece of Fulbert, a canon of Notre-Dame), Héloïse was also brilliant and beautiful. Abélard, who had never before felt the slightest interest in any woman, found Héloïse utterly irresistible. "All on fire with love for her," he carefully plotted his way into Héloïse's inner circle, offering his services as her tutor. Fulbert was overwhelmed. After all, Abélard was by now the most famous teacher in France. Completely unsuspicious, Héloïse's uncle readily agreed to let out rooms to Abélard in his own house, in the shadow of Notre-Dame.

You can still see the site of Fulbert's house at 9-11 Quai aux Fleurs, 4th, in the heart of the old Cloister Quarter to the north of Notre-Dame. There, two medallions representing the lovers gaze out from above the doors. This was a substantial property, stretching about halfway along the eastern side of tiny Rue des Chantres, from Rue Chanoinesse to the remains of the Gallo-Roman wall that still encircled Paris. Unlike the typically cramped houses of the time, it afforded Abélard and his beloved a degree of privacy.

Héloïse soon became as smitten with Abélard as he was

Héloïse   *Abélard*

with her, and before long the two were engaged in a passionate love affair. Quite literally, Abélard couldn't keep his hands off of her. Besotted with Héloïse, Abélard lost sleep as well as interest in teaching. His students at Notre-Dame complained of neglect, while the love songs he wrote became hits in student hangouts throughout the Cité.

Fulbert seems to have been the only person in Paris who didn't know about the affair. But when Héloïse became pregnant, even Fulbert realized what had been going on. Abélard promptly spirited her away to Brittany, where she gave birth to a son. Fulbert was furious, but grudgingly allowed the lovers to wed. Then he took his revenge, sending thugs to seize and castrate Abélard.

It was a shocking retaliation, even by medieval standards, plunging Héloïse into despair. At Abélard's urging, she became a nun, but never ceased to yearn for him. Abélard in turn entered a monastery, but promptly stirred up one disastrous confrontation after another.

For many dismal years, the two did not even communicate. But at length, after learning that Héloïse's convent was in need of a new home, Abélard unexpectedly offered up the teaching hermitage of Le Paraclet that he had established in Champagne. She accepted, and they met for the first time since the tragedy. It was a difficult encounter, in which Abélard insisted that Héloïse forget the past. Reluctantly, she came to accept his advice and, in time, became a renowned abbess. (In a footnote to their love affair, their son—raised in Brittany—may have become an abbot.)

Abélard returned to teaching in Paris, establishing a school in the vicinity of the present Sorbonne. His school, along with those of Notre-Dame and the nearby abbey of Saint-Victor, gave Paris a concentration of educational riches that within a century would lead to the founding of the University of Paris. No trace of Abélard's school remains, and even the Notre-Dame of his day has been replaced by Bishop Sully's magnificent twelfth-century creation. Still, pockets of Abélard's Paris have survived the centuries.

On the Left Bank, search out the tiny streets around the medieval church of Saint-Julien-le-Pauvre. On the Ile de la Cité, north of Rue du Cloître-Notre-Dame, wander the ancient Cloister Quarter, with its winding lanes and astonishing conjunction of rooftops. The corner of Rue des Chantres at Rue des Ursins, by Fulbert's house, is particularly evocative of Abélard's Paris, as are the medieval canons' houses at 22 and 24 Rue Chanoinesse. At 6 Rue de la Colombe, you may even make out remains of the Gallo-Roman wall that Abélard would have seen as he made his rounds.

Peace continued to elude Abélard—although in the end, it was his insistence on applying reason to theology rather than his scandalous love life that did him in. He dared to raise dangerous questions, and eventually he was condemned for heresy. Misunderstood and shattered, this powerful and original thinker went into severe decline following his condemnation, and soon died.

Grieving bitterly for him, Héloïse brought his body to Le Paraclet. There, at her own death, she was buried by his side. Following the Revolution and Le Paraclet's destruction, these tragic and endlessly fascinating lovers at last returned to Paris, the city where their love began.

They now lie side-by-side in Père-Lachaise cemetery, in a bower of trees. You will find their tomb to the right of the main entrance, where their final resting place continues to draw flowers from a steady stream of lovers and strangers who—despite the passage of nine centuries—know their story and wish them well.

4.

Pathways to the Past

CENTURIES AGO, WHEN THE SECOND MILLENNIUM WAS young and Paris was still recovering from the Vikings, a narrow pathway ran along the Left Bank, connecting the two great monasteries of Saint-Victor and Saint-Germain-des-Prés. Over the years, this well-used pathway became a road, whose course—much of it untouched by Baron Haussmann and his successors—you can still follow today.

The abbey of Saint-Victor no longer exists, although traces of this once-powerful center of learning remain in odd pockets around the University of Paris' Jussieu campus (5th). Tiny Rue Saint-Victor—a sunken and obviously aged remnant of Old Paris—is a piece of the ancient roadway leading to the old abbey. You can pick up the trail here and follow it via Rue Monge and Rue Lagrange to lively little Rue Galande and Square René-Viviani. Or you can take a slight detour, via little

Rue de Bièvre and Rue de la Bûcherie, past what once was the abbey's mill and back door.

Long ago, the monks of Saint-Victor diverted the course of the River Bièvre to water their extensive gardens and power a mill. This mill was located at about where today's Rue de Bièvre joins the Seine, and anyone wishing to reach it had to cross a small bridge called the Poncel. Undoubtedly many along the busy lane connecting this mill with the Petit Pont repeatedly made this journey. This well-traveled road, now the Rue de la Bûcherie (formerly Boucherie), was for centuries a noisy thoroughfare crammed with students and tradesmen. But today—along with its neighbors, the Rue de Bièvre and tiny Rue des Grands-Degrés—it has thankfully emerged from long years of overcrowding and neglect to become one of the most quietly romantic quarters of Paris.

Take a look at nearby Rue Galande, representing quite a different slice of the past. This narrow lane, which lies along an early Roman roadway to the south, has for centuries been jammed with tavern-seekers, loiterers, and travelers. Traditionally, many of the quarter's numerous students congregated here, and while doubtless some of them were up to no good, a respectable number were simply trying to get to classes in the Rue du Fouarre, just beyond. Here, in the early Middle Ages, students met in the open air, sitting on bundles of straw as they listened to their lecturers.

Both Rue Galande and Rue de la Bûcherie will take you to the Square René-Viviani, with its splendid views of Notre-Dame. The Square boasts a hoary robinia tree (Robinia pseudoacacia),

Fourteenth-century stone carving of St. Julien and his wife rowing
Christ across the Seine; 42 Rue Galande

reputedly planted in 1602 and easily one of the oldest trees in
Paris. But the Square's real treasure is the adjoining twelfth-
century church of Saint-Julien-le-Pauvre, built on the ruins of its
far-older predecessor. Here students assembled during the University of Paris' earliest days, to hold their disputations. Here, as
well, centuries of students attended morning Mass before rush-
ing off to classes. The church's twelfth-century façade has crum-
bled, exposing an ancient well to the right of the entry, but jagged
remnants of the original still hauntingly remain.

On the far side of Square René-Viviani, Rue de la
Bûcherie crosses Rue du Petit Pont, a major thoroughfare
that quickly becomes Rue Saint-Jacques—once the major
Roman road to Orléans. Here, long ago, a fortified gate

defended the tiny Petit Pont, which until the late fourteenth century was the only southern entry into the Cité. This diminutive bridge had quite a different look then, with narrow shops and houses lining its sides, and teachers holding forth to students jammed around their doorsteps. Even then, traffic across this bridge and onto the broad road to Orléans was heavy, with the lucky ones, on horseback, shoving their way through crowds of carts and foot-traffic.

The Orléans road was a major dividing point between traffic to the east, heading for Saint-Victor, and traffic making its way westward, toward the abbey and village of Saint-Germain-des-Prés. As if to underscore this distinction, the Rue de la Boucherie long ago changed its name as it crossed this roadway, becoming the Rue de la Huchette on the other side.

Since medieval times, little Rue de la Huchette has been a boisterous place, lined with cookshops and taverns. For centuries it was also notorious for its cutpurses—the equivalent of pickpockets, who were busy slashing and seizing money-purses long before pockets were invented. This narrow and colorful street has been considerably cleaned up, but the Mediterranean kebab joints that now proliferate here are a gaudy reminder of an indecorous past.

This entire quarter, including the equally ancient Rue Xavier-Privas and Rue de la Harpe, almost succumbed to Baron Haussmann's wrecking ball but was saved by events. Haussmann lost his job during the upheavals of 1870, putting an abrupt stop to his myriad works in progress, including a plan for gutting this old quarter. He destroyed the first buildings at the corner of Rue de la Huchette and Rue de la Harpe, where he was intent on major road-widening, but this was as far as he got. Fortunately, the rest of these remarkable old streets and alleys still remain.

Crossing Place Saint-Michel into the 6th arrondissement, you can pick up the continuation of the medieval pathway along the Rue Saint-André-des-Arts—originally called the Rue de Laas, because it crossed through the Clos de Laas, an extensive tract of land belonging to the abbey of Saint-Germain-des-Prés. Here you may want to detour to the Cour de Rohan, a series of three tiny and charming courtyards off Rue de l'Eperon and Rue du Jardinet. A particularly enchanting pocket of the past, the Cour de Rohan even contains a portion of Paris' old twelfth-century wall (take a close look at the terrace in the third and last courtyard). An entire tower from this wall spectacularly survives in the adjoining Cour du Commerce Saint-André (at No. 4), where the Catalonian tourist office has preserved it. The Cour du Commerce Saint-André, by the way, dates from the eighteenth century, not the twelfth, but nonetheless evokes a distant age.

From Rue Saint-André-des-Arts, the medieval path continues onto Rue de Buci, a narrow street that curves down toward Boulevard Saint-Germain and the abbey's former entrance. Haussmann destroyed much of this neighborhood when he blasted the boulevard through, but some of Old Paris still remains. Where it doesn't, use your imagination— such as at the intersection of Rue de Buci and Boulevard Saint-Germain, where the medieval abbey set up its pillory (replaced, in the seventeenth century, by a prison), or at the nearby corner of Rue Gozlin and Rue des Ciseaux, where the fortified abbey's entrance once rose.

At the corner of tiny Passage de la Petite Boucherie and the Rue de l'Abbaye stands the sixteenth-century abbey palace, a remarkable brick-and-stone edifice that has recently been restored (it now houses the Institut Catholique de Paris). In the small park beside the church, you can find vestiges of the abbey's thirteenth-century Chapel of the Virgin, once located at 6 and 8 Rue de l'Abbaye.

The most important survivor is the abbey church of Saint-Germain-des-Prés itself, the oldest church in Paris. Its one remaining tower dates from the turn of the first millennium,

Saint-Germain-des-Prés

and its Romanesque nave is only slightly younger. Small marble columns from the church's sixth-century predecessor decorate the upper level of the choir. If you look closely inside the Chapelle de Saint-Symphorian, to the right of the entry, you can see vestiges of that sixth-century basilica.

Rest for a while at Deux Magots, across the way, to contemplate your journey. You have traversed more than eight centuries, along byways already worn deep by countless carts and footsteps long before Columbus was born.

How does it feel to be a time traveler?

III

CASCADES and CURRENTS

5.

Lost River

ONCE UPON A TIME, NOT SO VERY LONG AGO, THERE were two rivers in Paris—the Seine and the Bièvre. The Seine bisected Paris from east to west, while the little Bièvre entered Paris from the south, winding its way through the Left Bank before depositing its waters in the Seine.

The Seine remains one of the glories of Paris, but the Bièvre has disappeared. Few today know its history or know that it still flows through Paris—underground, in pipes. And few know the delights of following its original course, from the 13th to the 5th arrondissement, exploring a little-known part of Paris and discovering unexpected river-fed bowers along the way.

Once a bucolic stream where, according to legend, beaver thrived (possibly giving the watercourse its name), for centuries the Bièvre merrily meandered through a countryside dotted with ancient watermills and rustic villages. Within Paris, its waters flowed past mills and gardens, its tree-lined banks providing shade and beauty.

But then a series of ecological disasters struck. Jean Gobelin, a dyer, may not have been the first to sully the Bièvre's pristine waters, but he surely was the most influential.

Attracted to the Bièvre by its minerals, suitable for fixing dyes, Gobelin set up shop in what is now the 13ᵗʰ arrondissement. By the seventeenth century, this foray had blossomed into the renowned Gobelins tapestry workshops, attracting a plethora of tanners and dyers to the neighborhood. By the eighteenth century, Paris' Bièvre had grown dark and polluted, and even its upstream waters suffered from considerable contamination after Christophe Philippe Oberkampf began to manufacture his famed toile print fabrics in the little riverside village of Jouy en Josas.

Industrialization completed what the early polluters began, and by the nineteenth century the Bièvre had become little more than a fetid sewer that coursed its way through the most poverty-stricken reaches of Paris. No one objected when the city of Paris dealt with this horror by gradually relegating it underground.

Since then, the industrial slums through which the Bièvre flowed have made way for a far more welcoming environment, and now a series of pleasant parks and intriguing nooks dot the stream's original course. This has led to considerable civic interest in bringing back the Bièvre, and today a growing group of environmentalists and civic leaders have banded together to liberate the much-abused river. City Hall has responded positively, offering the prospect of substantial action within the next few years to restore a portion of this historic waterway.

In the meantime, you needn't wait to enjoy a walk along the Bièvre. Although the living river has disappeared from view, you can still follow its winding course, wandering through some interesting off-the-beaten-path neighborhoods and making some delightful discoveries along the way.

Originating in Guyancourt, near Versailles, the Bièvre enters Paris through Parc Kellermann, on the site of what once were the Thiers fortifications—the last and largest of Paris' former walls. This bristling set of defenses was torn down in 1919, leaving a wide band of available land around the city's circumference. The Périphérique (Paris' beltway) eventually took much of this, but not all. In the 14th arrondissement, the remaining ribbon provided ample space for the attractive Cité Internationale Universitaire de Paris, while in the 13th arrondissement, more than a dozen acres along the Bièvre became Parc Kellermann—one of the loveliest and least known parks in Paris.

Make your way from the Porte d'Italie Métro to the park's entrance, on Boulevard Kellermann, and you will soon find yourself in another world, one most fittingly enhanced by water. From the formal French gardens at the park's entrance, descend through lush greenery to a romantic setting punctuated by weeping willows, streams, and pools. Most dramatic of all is the monumental waterfall that plummets down a high retaining wall before pouring into a succession of rocky basins. These in turn flow into a small lake, from which jets of water spray skyward.

The Bièvre flowed freely here until the 1930s, and it still runs beneath your feet—through a large conduit, the Collecteur Pascal. Centuries ago, right about where you are now standing, some enterprising Parisians divided the Bièvre into two roughly parallel streams. By banking up an artificial

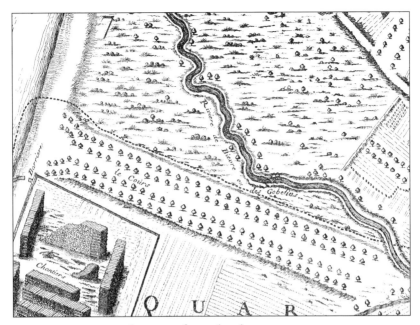

The Bièvre from Plan de Paris, 1710

riverbed, higher than the original, they cleverly provided power for a number of watermills further downstream. The Collecteur Pascal follows this upper course, skirting to the right of the playing field and crossing beneath Boulevard Kellermann to Rue de l'Interne-Loeb.

Since you cannot cross Boulevard Kellermann here as easily as does the river, you may prefer to follow the course of the lower Bièvre along Rue de la Poterne-des-Peupliers to the Poterne des Peupliers (Poplar Gate), where it passed through the now-vanished Thiers fortifications. The poplars that once lined the riverbank still border this narrow thoroughfare, while the viaduct under what now is Boulevard Kellermann contains some vestiges of the old walls.

Continuing along the lower Bièvre's winding course, follow

Rue des Peupliers uphill—yes, uphill—to the pleasantly old-fashioned Place de l'Abbé-Georges-Henocque, turning briefly aside to enjoy the picturesque enclave of pastel houses at Rue du Docteur-Leray. Here the Collecteur Pascal (which you have been shadowing) cuts directly to the west, abandoning the serpentine riverbed of the upper Bièvre for a slightly more direct route. An interesting half-timbered house marks the spot.

Nearby, at 98 Rue du Moulin-des-Prés, is the approximate site of an old watermill that once operated on the upper Bièvre. If you find this a strange location for a watermill—after all, how could a river flow up the hill you've been climbing since Boulevard Kellermann?—be assured that the mill's actual site was about sixty feet beneath your feet. Rivers don't run uphill, even in Paris. Instead, the landscape in this part of town has changed dramatically during the past century, thanks to some massive earthmoving. Just to give you an idea: Rue du Moulin-des-Prés once crossed far below Rue de Tolbiac, which formed an impressive viaduct high above the Bièvre.

If you follow present-day Rue du Moulin-des-Prés to Rue de Tolbiac, you will find the Square des Peupliers, a tiny jewel of a cul-de-sac at 72 Rue du Moulin-des-Prés. Shade-drenched and bordered with wisteria-covered houses, this cobbled lane lies at the point where both branches of the Bièvre bumped up against the rocky Butte-aux-Cailles (Quail Hill). From here they looped south, the lower course following Rue de la Fontaine-à-Mulard to Place de Rungis.

Long ago, when winter came and the river froze, young people came to skate in these pond-filled lowlands, known as la

Glacière. Others came to chop up portions of the frozen water into blocks of ice, which they stored in ice-houses (*glacières*). Eventually the marshy lands of la Glacière were filled in to make room for new housing, but happily this included the charmingly eccentric Cité Florale. Located immediately to the west of Place de Rungis, and just a few minutes' walk from Parc Montsouris, the Cité Florale is a village of tiny houses so picturesque that one is amazed that it has remained relatively unknown. Enter by Rue Brillat-Savarin and wander down the flower-named lanes.

If you're paying attention to your map, you'll note the Bièvre's imprint everywhere—on the placement and curvature of streets as well as on place names summoning up images of trees, flowers, and country mills. From Place de Rungis, the lower streambed curves around what now is the Cité Florale via Rue Brillat-Savarin to Rue Wurtz. Along the way, you'll find other jewels, such as la Petite-Alsace (10 Rue Daviel), an enclave of blue and cream half-timbered houses, and Rue Le Dantec, a lovely old street at the base of the quiet and village-like Butte-aux-Cailles.

Crossing under la Petite-Alsace, the upper Bièvre met up with its sister branch at Boulevard Auguste-Blanqui. Here the two passed through a double watergate in the old toll walls (demolished in 1860) and once again divided. The higher stream flowed along what now is Rue Edmond-Gondinet, where it passed another watermill (the Moulin de Croulebarbe, at the corner of Rue Corvisart), while the lower stream ran along what now is Rue Paul-Gervais. Together, the two arms enclosed a lush enclave that once provided kitchen plots for Gobelins workers and now is the Square René-le-Gall, a secret garden dating (like Parc Kellermann) from the 1930s. This place has a history: almost two centuries ago, Victor Hugo frequented the rustic tavern that still stands at 41 Rue de Croulebarbe, along what once was a riverbank path. Nowadays this tavern (currently a restaurant) overlooks Square René-le-Gall's gently flowing water and densely forested interior—a haven of peace and greenery on the banks of the river's ancient course.

From Rue de Croulebarbe, follow the upper Bièvre's curve along Rue Berbier-du-Mets, behind the Gobelins workshops. While here, you might want to take a look at the Hôtel de la Reine Blanche (at 17 and 19 Rue des Gobelins), twin Gothic mansions dating from around the year 1500—among the oldest in Paris.

Much like the Collecteur Pascal, you will find it easier to cross Boulevard Arago at Rue Pascal, following both streams' approximate course to the busy intersection at the foot of Montagne Sainte-Geneviève, where Rue Mouffetard—complete with its famous street market—begins its climb. Here, where the old Roman road to Lyon crossed the Bièvre, two medieval mills—the Moulin Saint-Marcel and the Petit-Moulin—ground wheat into flour. And here, at last, the two arms of the Bièvre rejoined into one.

Skirting Montagne Sainte-Geneviève, the newly unified river plunged onward, toward the Seine. Originally it followed a course that took it along what now is Square Adanson and between Rue Buffon and Rue Poliveau, where it ran past another mill (the

Moulin Coupeau) at Rue Geoffroy-Saint-Hilaire. From there it flowed through the annex of the Museum of Natural History and beneath the curve of Rue Nicolas-Houël to its final destination, just upriver from the present Pont d'Austerlitz.

There it might have stayed, had it not been for the monks of the abbey of Saint-Victor, who in 1151 received permission to re-route it through their lands to irrigate their extensive gardens and power a mill. Virtually nothing remains of this once-powerful abbey, located on the present site of the University of Paris' Jussieu campus, but you can follow the Bièvre's artificial course—through the Jardin des Plantes and along Rue Jussieu—to where it emptied, just downstream of the Pont de l'Archevêché. En route, you will find one of the most exciting archeological discoveries of recent years—the Arche de la Bièvre, marking the place where the re-routed stream passed through Paris' twelfth-century walls on its way to the Seine.

Built about a half-century after the Bièvre's alteration, these moated and towered fortifications completely encircled the city. Yet what to do about the recently redirected river? The monks certainly were not interested in putting it back, which left the king's engineers with the task of constructing a gate capable of letting in the Bièvre while keeping out the enemy.

They succeeded, creating a dramatic stone arch guarded by a portcullis, through which the water—but not the enemy—could enter. In time, this wall lost its usefulness, and the arch disappeared under the dirt and rubble of the centuries. Few even remembered that it existed until a decade ago, when excavations for a post office at 30 Rue du Cardinal-Lemoine (at the corner of Rue des Ecoles) uncovered this eight hundred-year-old treasure. Now carefully restored, it can be seen (via an underground parking garage) on the first Wednesday afternoon of each month, except August. (For further information, inquire at the post office about the "Visite de l'Arche".)

Two centuries after Philip Augustus' engineers created the magnificent Arche de la Bièvre, Charles V incorporated the river's waters into a new set of defensive moats around the old medieval walls. Responding to this challenge, the monks got to work upstream and dug yet another canal, leaving the moats and first canal to fester. This unhealthy state of affairs lasted until the reign of Louis XIV, who ordered both canals to be filled. The river then returned to its original course—until the nineteenth century, when it was buried and ignominiously dumped into the Paris sewer system.

Still, for more than two hundred years, the Bièvre was content to follow the first canal that the monks of Saint-Victor made for it—through the city wall and along little Rue Saint-Victor to its final destination, at the tip of Rue de Bièvre. This narrow lane, just off Place Maubert, is steeped in history—a fitting place to end your journey. Admiring these wonderful old houses, it is difficult to imagine that once, like so much of the route through which the Bièvre passed, this ancient street was a slum. Completely rejuvenated, Rue de Bièvre now is a fashionable district where former President François Mitterand made his home, at No. 22.

A happy ending—at least for the areas through which the Bièvre once flowed. But what about the river itself? Could it once again flow sweetly through the city of Paris? Upstream, thanks to the coordinated efforts of the towns through which it passes, the revived Bièvre now flows *à ciel ouvert* from its source in Guyancourt to the suburbs of Paris, with pleasant riverbank paths along the way. This would be impossible in Paris' dense urban setting, but the river could be revived and brought back to the surface in selected spots. Of these, the sites that have attracted the most interest are Parc Kellermann, Square René-le-Gall and adjoining Rue Berbier-du-Mets, and the annex of the Museum of Natural History.

Bringing these ambitious plans to life still lies in the future. But it is quite possible that someday, as you walk down Rue Berbier-du-Mets, you may find yourself strolling alongside an ancient tree-lined river whose waters flow beneath small footbridges that carry pedestrians to their front doors. A dream, perhaps, but not an impossible one. In the meantime, take a few hours to explore the Bièvre's old course. You will be traveling through history, and you will undoubtedly enjoy where it takes you.

6.

Enchanted
Canal

OUR DAY BEGAN AT PLACE DE LA BATAILLE-DE-Stalingrad (straddling the 10th and 19th arrondissements), a gritty neighborhood in the heart of a working-class area known as the "Red suburbs." We had come to look at a remnant of the past, a remarkable two-hundred-year-old rotunda installed as a tollhouse during the waning days of the *Ancien Régime*.

"Don't miss this!" my husband called, as I gazed out across the rotunda's park to the Bassin de la Villette beyond. Following his voice up and over a hillock and through some trees, I found myself at the edge of the Canal Saint-Martin, where a barge heading out of the Bassin de la Villette was preparing to enter the first lock—not a pleasure craft, to be sure, but a gravel-hauler, deadheading home.

This clearly was a family enterprise, for Madame was steering while her husband took charge of the ropes. A battery of flowerpots gave an unexpected feminine touch to the pilothouse, while a well-manicured poodle trotted about, checking out how everyone was doing. If it hadn't been for the time it took for the locks to drain, we would have followed our barge's progress into Paris. Instead, we decided to follow the canal on our own.

Canal Saint-Martin, completed in the 1820s, was designed to extend two other canals, the Ourcq and the Saint-Denis (which meet just above the Bassin de la Villette), into a waterway cutting across one of the Seine's many wide-ranging loops, linking it with the river Ourcq. Although Napoléon had originally conceived of this canal network as a means of bringing the Ourcq's waters to the fountains of Paris, it remained pristine only briefly. Soon, the Industrial Revolution flooded in, blighting everything it touched. Where there once had been grassy banks, there now stood warehouses and foundries. Abject poverty soon followed, accompanied by radical politics and a readiness for mob uprisings.

Eventually Baron Haussmann ordered the southern third of Canal Saint-Martin covered over, between Place de la République and Place de la Bastille. But while government troops could now march unhindered into this hellhole, little else changed. Poverty and blight continued a century longer, until land shortage and soaring property values in western Paris encouraged a new look at this neglected area to the east. By the late 1970s, cleanup had begun.

The Canal Saint-Martin that my husband and I encountered that sunny Sunday afternoon was, fortunately, a far different place from its woebegone predecessor. While Place de la Bataille-de-Stalingrad is still down-at-the-heels, the canal itself is an attractive daytime destination, drawing a happy throng of couples and families. The street rally we encountered near the beginning of our three-mile journey was a staged one, with singers costumed as revolutionary *sans-culottes* swirling a red flag. We applauded with the rest of the crowd as a *chanteuse*—accompanied by dramatic thrumming on the bass—urged liberty and revolution for oppressed peoples everywhere. And then, after passing up the group's CD, we went our way, feeling that we had just witnessed a little slice of the past.

As we discovered, the canal drops eighty feet before joining the Seine at the Bassin de l'Arsenal (4th and 12th), requiring nine locks to do the job. It also takes a significant bend to circumvent the Hôpital Saint-Louis, which still retains its seventeenth-century quadrangle (open on weekdays; enter through 2 Place du Docteur-Alfred-Fournier, on Rue Bichat, 10th).

After walking over to take a look at the old quadrangle, we returned to the canal, glad to be embraced once again by the splendid trees shading this portion of the embankment, their reflections mirrored in the darkened water. Although only six feet deep, the canal here is almost ninety feet wide—enough to give an enchanted feel to this last bit before it plunges under cover. Responding to the lush stillness, voices around us became subdued, while several teenagers seemed content to sit quietly along the canal's edge, feet dangling over the water.

We approached the end of our waterside walk at the Rue du Faubourg-du-Temple, as we entered gardens and playgrounds that extended from block to block down the center of Boulevard Jules-Ferry (which becomes Boulevard Richard-Lenoir), over the canal. In this lively family scene, neighbors were congregating to chat, enjoy the flowers, and watch the children play, oblivious of the canal that flowed directly beneath their feet. In fact, if it hadn't been for the occasional mysterious-looking ventilation dome rising out of the earth, we would have entirely forgotten that a canal existed at all.

We found the gardens making way for an outdoor market, which continued all the way to the Place de la Bastille. There the canal reappeared, this time in the form of a marina—the sparkling boat basin of the Paris Arsenal. As we climbed down the embankment and made our way to the Seine—well ahead of the barge we had left behind—we congratulated ourselves on our new walk, and decided that the next sunny Sunday afternoon we had in Paris, we would do it all over again.

The King's Water Machine

WHENEVER THE SUN KING, LOUIS XIV, TOOK A vacation from his court at Versailles, he usually headed to nearby Marly. There, freed from stultifying Versailles etiquette, he relaxed and enjoyed himself, indulging his taste for the hunt and limiting his guest list to an elite few, who could fit in the small pavilions that bordered his exquisite little chateau.

The king dearly loved Marly, and he created a small paradise here, complete with manicured gardens and groves. But more than anything, he created at Marly a fairyland of water—of sprays, jets, fountains, and cascades that dripped, flowed, and poured into the large pools at the park's center. Courtiers were suitably impressed—as the king had intended. Those who understood the mechanics required to deliver all that water to the king's playground were even more in awe of what the Sun King had accomplished.

The extraordinary device that made this extravaganza possible was a huge hydraulic machine, the Machine de Marly, that pumped enormous quantities of water up the steep slopes of the Seine to the vast water wonderlands of Marly and Versailles. The brainchild of a well-connected lawyer, Arnold de Ville, and his mechanically adept associate, Rennequin Sualem, this magnificent machine was inaugurated in 1684. It represented a quantum leap into the technological future, defying gravity with a dizzying array of pumps, pipes, rods, and paddle wheels that lifted large portions of the Seine some five hundred feet up the hillside to an equally magisterial aqueduct.

Whether or not the Sun King understood the major push he had given the development of hydraulics, he was vastly pleased with the results. The fountains of Versailles, which had sputtered ignominiously for years, now shot up to full height, while the waterworks at Marly flowed copiously. Moreover, the creaking, clanking Marly engine managed to do its job for well over a century before serious attention had to be given to replacing it. No longer a mere plaything of royalty, it had become an indispensable part of daily life, supplying drinking water for a string of neighboring towns above the Seine.

With the old machine on its last legs, a series of engineers went to work to revive it, introducing updated hydraulics, steam, and, eventually, electrification to keep the giant wheels turning. But even new techniques had their limits, and by the middle of the twentieth century the Marly Machine had reached the end of its useful life. Having survived almost three hundred years, this enormous white elephant—once considered the Eighth Wonder of the World—went to the junkyard in 1968.

Yet not all traces of the Sun King's wondrous machine have completely vanished; in fact, the Machine de Marly has left a lasting footprint along this inviting stretch of the Seine. Stand on the small bridge to the Ile de la Loge, just west of the Bougival bridge, and look out to where the huge paddle wheels once churned. Better still, follow the dramatic uphill route that the Machine's pipes took, from the Seine to Marly, along the old Chemin de la Machine (also known as the Chemin de la Mi-Côte). Halfway up the hillside you will find remnants of the Ferme de la Mi-Côte, the mid-level pumping station with crumbling farm and support buildings that Impressionist painter Alfred Sisley immortalized. A bit farther on, you will be rewarded on clear days with a spectacular view of Paris.

At the top of the hill, this footpath turns into the Rue de la Machine, an elegant tree-lined stretch that extends past the chateau bestowed by Louis XV on his mistress, Madame du Barry. Across from the Pavillon des Eaux (where the Marly Machine's inventor, Arnold de Ville, once lived), tiny Place Ernest-Dreux leads to buildings that originally housed the Marly Machine's foundry and, many years later, painter Pierre-Auguste Renoir and composer Kurt Weill.

From the center of the still-rustic village of Voisins, Avenue Saint-Martin will take you to the Marly Aqueduct, that stunning structure built to carry the waters of the Seine on the last leg of their journey to Marly. This eye-catching series of thirty-six arches, bookended between massive towers, will in turn lead you to the Parc de Marly and the Musée Promenade. This intimate museum preserves the art, architectural plans, and a variety of colorful remnants of the Sun King's long-vanished chateau, as well as a fascinating working model of the Marly Machine itself. Outside the museum's door, you will find the remains of those many splendid pools and fountains that once relied on the machine's pumping power. (Their sculptures have vanished, but you can find some of the most important, including the famous Marly horses, in the Louvre's Cour Marly. Reproductions of the Marly horses also grace the Place de la Concorde.)

Do as the museum's name suggests and wander the pathways that Louis XIV himself once strolled. Time and the ravages of Revolution may have erased his elaborate architecture, but they cannot destroy the peaceful beauty of this setting—nor its link to the Seine through that captivating wonder, the Machine de Marly.

NOTE: To follow the Chemin de la Machine/Chemin de la Mi-Côte (a ten to fifteen minute climb), take Bus No. 258 from La Défense to "La Machine" stop in Bougival (on N13). Return via SNCF to Gare Saint-Lazare from Marly-le-Roi, the picturesque town adjoining the Parc de Marly. (For a downhill walk, start at Marly-le-Roi and end in Bougival.) The Bougival entrance to the Chemin de la Machine/Chemin de la Mi-Côte is located on the eastern side of what still is a pumping station (uphill pipes are visible to the rear).

IV

SMALL TREASURES

8.

The Oldest House in Paris

WHEN BARON HAUSSMANN REMADE THE FACE OF PARIS, he relegated much of the medieval city to the wrecking ball. Yet despite his efforts, pockets of the past still remain, ready for discovery. If you are willing to search, you can still find them—including some of the oldest houses in Paris.

Actually, there are several contenders for the title, all of them to be found on the Right Bank rather than the Left, near the historic church of Saint-Gervais-Saint-Protais (4th) and the former abbey church of Saint-Martin-des-Champs (now part of the Musée des Arts et Métiers, 3rd). They reflect the division, already well-established by the twelfth century, between the university on the Left Bank, a burgeoning commercial district on the Right Bank, and the seat of government (the royal palace) on the Ile de la Cité.

Take the house of Nicolas Flamel. The name may mean something to you, as he shows up rather prominently in the first Harry Potter story, and Victor Hugo refers ominously to him in *The Hunchback of Notre-Dame*. Flamel has gone down in history, or in the shadows of history, as a dedicated alchemist who discovered the Philosophers' Stone and its secret of eternal life. Since the Philosophers' Stone was also capable of turning base metals into gold, subsequent seekers have not been surprised to learn that Flamel was a wealthy man.

In addition to any time he may have put in at his laboratory, Flamel was a successful manuscript copyist and dealer as well as a major community benefactor. In 1407 he built the sturdy stone structure at what is now 51 Rue de Montmorency (3rd), setting aside the top stories as a kind of homeless shelter, while turning the ground floor into a money-making tavern (which now houses a popular little restaurant, the Auberge Nicolas Flamel). If you look carefully, you can make out some of the original carvings on the façade, including angels, Flamel's initials, and a Latin inscription invoking the inhabitants' prayers.

Flamel, who only asked that his impoverished lodgers pray for him and his wife, was also a generous benefactor to the Church of Saint-Jacques-la-Boucherie, whose tower still remains at the corner of Rue de Rivoli and Boulevard de Sébastopol (4th). In remembrance of his good works, two tiny streets to the immediate north of the Tower of Saint-Jacques were named for him and his wife, Pernelle. Rue Nicolas-Flamel and Rue Pernelle (4ᵗʰ) still exist, and the spot where they cross provides a wonderful view of the dramatically lit tower by night.

The house of Nicolas Flamel is certainly the oldest stone house in Paris, but the nearby half-timbered structure at 3 Rue Volta (3ʳᵈ), located in back of Saint-Martin-des-Champs, was long considered the oldest house in Paris.

Saint-Martin-des-Champs, which faces the old Roman road (now Rue Saint-Martin) from Paris to the sea, dates from the twelfth and thirteenth centuries, with roots that go back long before that. Like other abbey churches in the area, a small village grew up around its protective walls, and 3 Rue Volta may once have belonged to a leading dignitary of the village of Saint-Martin. Despite its obvious age, this contender's title has recently been challenged: instead of dating from around the year 1300, experts now say that the house that presently occupies 3 Rue Volta may be a seventeenth-century replacement for the original.

The last two rivals for the oldest-house prize thrust up their half-timbered structures at 11 and 13 Rue François-Miron (4ᵗʰ), behind the church of Saint-Gervais-Saint-Protais, whose tower foundations date from the thirteenth century, and whose history extends several centuries before that. As with 3 Rue Volta, these houses line an ancient roadway of Roman origins, this one connecting Paris to points east.

The tall gabled structures of 11 and 13 Rue François-Miron date from the fourteenth century and give perhaps the best feeling of what medieval Paris looked like. Although various ordinances and age itself greatly altered their appearance over the centuries, they have recently been restored to their former glory, with plaques proclaiming that No. 11 is the House at the Sign of the Mower (reaper), while No. 13 is the House at the Sign of the Sheep. At the corner, an old sign for the Relais Saint-Gervais adds to the atmosphere of this special part of Paris.

11-13 Rue François-Miron

These are of course small treasures, in a city that fairly bursts with riches of a larger order. But for those who value the many layers of history upon which present-day Paris is built, these remnants of the past are a delight to discover.

9.

Hidden Chapel

To begin with, Saint-Aignan isn't easy to find. Following small clues, I stood before the locked gate at 19 Rue des Ursins (4th) and peered inside, trying to find some evidence of a chapel there. But all I could see was an empty courtyard. No sign of a chapel anywhere, not even a tiny one.

Still, I knew there was a twelfth-century chapel somewhere in the neighborhood, one with a particularly interesting pedigree. Back in the early 1120s, almost nine centuries ago, a brilliant ecclesiastical and political figure by the name of Etienne de Garlande had built it virtually as an adjunct to his house, in what then was the cloister of Notre-Dame. Garlande, who was archdeacon of the cathedral, had risen through political ranks as well to become chancellor to the king. The chapel of Saint-Aignan, which joined a cluster of other churches and chapels on this eastern end of the Ile de la Cité, was all that a man of his power and wealth could make it—a miniature masterpiece of early Parisian architecture.

I knew something else about Saint-Aignan. Rather daringly, Garlande had built it just outside the ancient Gallo-Roman city wall. By Garlande's time, barbarian and Viking attacks were a thing of the past, and King Louis VI had effectively restrained marauding noblemen, but the Seine still flooded regularly, and anything beyond the old walls was particularly vulnerable. Nonetheless, Garlande boldly filled in the marshy area to the north and built his chapel there—the first structure to breach the old Gallo-Roman wall.

So, in my hunt for the chapel, I followed the old Gallo-Roman wall. I knew that a nice chunk of it crossed Rue de la Colombe (you can see the marking in the pavement just out-side No. 6). According to old maps, it then took the most direct route eastward, which in today's terms meant that it went directly between Rue des Ursins and Rue Chanoinesse, two of the oldest streets on the island. Rue des Ursins, which lies well below the adjoining Quai aux Fleurs, remains close to what the island's level had been when Saint-Aignan was built. It's an old street that has gone through many names, but I knew that my prize lay somewhere in that knot of buildings at its western end.

Everything pointed to that courtyard, but I couldn't seem to get beyond its gates. Usually, the street was deserted. But one evening as I strolled past, I saw a woman emerge from a nearby house. Was there a chapel located in that courtyard?, I asked her.

Oh, yes, she assured me, and pointed toward one of the houses.

Baffled, I tried to find out more, but she got going at such a clip that I (and my French) couldn't keep up. Suddenly she said,

"Ah, there is the person you should speak with, Madame." And, indeed, rounding the corner was another woman. After introductions all around, I explained that I was an historian who was greatly interested in the chapel. She replied that, most unfortunately, it was not open to the public. And then, with a little twinkle, she suddenly asked, "But would you like to see it?"

Would I! As I expressed my profound gratitude, she unlocked the gate and led me across the courtyard. Then—with a little smile, as if we were in a mutual conspiracy—she unlocked a small door into what at first looked like a cellar. Could this possibly be where the old chapel was hiding?

But, of course. It turns out that after the Revolution (which stripped Saint-Aignan of its ecclesiastical purposes), the chapel fell on hard times. Sadly, it became a storeroom and stable for a house, with both structures plastered over to look like one building. That could have been the end of Saint-Aignan, but fortunately, a recent owner recognized the chapel's worth and gave it back to the diocese. After cleaning and careful restoration, it now serves as a chapel for the nearby Seminaire de Paris.

I stepped inside. It was dark, barely lit with lamps strategically placed to illuminate the structural elements and carvings. Though small in size, its Romanesque vaults reach some fourteen feet above the floor. After the Revolution, an internal wall was built across the nave, and steps now lead up through a doorway into the equally diminutive second room (overall, the whole chapel measures about twenty-one feet wide by thirty-three feet long). But it was the room where I now was standing that absorbed my attention.

It is difficult to convey what it feels like to be in such a space. Despite its long years of desecration, Saint-Aignan radiates an unusual amount of tranquility. The blessed absence of tour groups undoubtedly contributes to the calm, but more than anything, Saint-Aignan seems to reflect the assuredness of a place of worship that has survived. Its beauty is in its strength, which its Romanesque arches clearly delineate. The Gothic (soon to arrive in Paris) was all about light and soaring, but this little chapel reminded me of the importance of being solidly rooted. The result is reassuringly intimate—perfectly rein- forced by the sculpture of the Virgin and Child against the east- ern wall. This is a reproduction; the original, dating from the fourteenth century, now graces the southeast pillar of Notre-Dame's transept. This one, too, is lovely.

There have been other changes as well—some the result of hardship, others the outcome of changing taste or the ravages of time. Once upon a time, there was a rounded apse where a flat wall now rises. A stained glass window depicting Saint Aignan has disappeared. The door through which I entered has been cut into the north wall (its inner side painted to camouflage it). Still, what is remarkable is how much remains.

First, there are those rounded Romanesque arches, sturdy and graceful relics that have survived the ages. And then there is the carving. Although time has eroded some of it, much has endured. Stylized leaves, cut confidently and deep, crown the capitals of the larger columns in the Corinthian manner. Only a master carver could have created these intricate beauties, and some think he must have been a Burgundian, trained in an abbey of Cluny workshop. By the time Garlande began to build his chapel, Cluniac style had come to represent the pinnacle of good taste.

Cluny had its detractors, of course. Saint Bernard of Clairvaux (an ecclesiastical and political power in his own right) didn't care for Cluny or its style, but Garlande enjoyed good relations with several Cluniac abbeys and didn't think much of Bernard. He may well have looked to Burgundy for a carver of renown. In any case, Garlande had both the eminence and the wealth to attract such talent to his door.

Whatever his identity, a talented carver seems to have been responsible for most of the sculpture in Saint-Aignan, including elements of some small carvings along a recently rediscovered portal on the chapel's southern wall. Another hand appears to have been responsible for the small faces within these medallions, which are less-deftly crafted, but show remarkable individuality.

This same hand, or hands, may also have been responsible for the somewhat crude but friendly array of animals that crown the smaller columns within the chapel, including a monkey, or monkey-like man, with a bulging tummy; a winged griffin (I thought it looked like a salamander, but apparently I'm wrong), and two friendly lions, their paws just touching. Someone had a good deal of fun with these figures, especially the monkey, which may have closely resembled an associate—possibly even one of the clerics.

Local craftsmen working with a Burgundian mentor? We will never know. But thanks to Saint-Aignan, we do know that quality carving had revived in the Paris area by the early twelfth century—much earlier than once thought. Indeed, Garlande had much to be proud of when his chapel was completed. He had built solidly, and with all the artistry that his position and wealth commanded.

Fortunately, his chapel of Saint-Aignan still survives—a deeply moving legacy from a distant past.

NOTE: Saint-Aignan is usually open during Paris' Journées du Patrimoine, on the third weekend of September.

Those Bad Beaumont Boys

BACK IN THE BAD OLD DAYS OF THE ELEVENTH CENTURY, when Paris was little more than a ghost town, chaos ruled and a freebooting nobility did pretty much as it pleased. Perhaps the most dangerous in those parts was Robert of Beaumont, lord of Monceau-Saint-Gervais—a title that gave him considerable clout over a large part of the Seine's Right Bank, at the king's very door.

Robert acquired this choice real estate around the year 1081 from his grandfather, the count of Meulan, whose lands were strategically situated along the Norman frontier. Having already hacked his way through Hastings and received the earldom of Leicester as his reward, Robert now became count of Meulan, with the Paris property included in the title. In another wind-fall, Robert's father retreated to the local monastery, adding his hefty Norman holdings to the son's portfolio.

Dust off your history books and recall that only a few years before, a duke of Normandy, William the Bastard, had become king of England—an uncomfortable fact for the struggling French monarchy. Then pull out a map and note how close Normandy is to Paris (about forty miles), the heart of the French king's domains. The French monarchy had been feeble for years, and the new Capetian monarchs had done little to reverse the trend. Now they faced the possibility of extinction at the hands of a Norman upstart who wore England's crown.

Paris had for some years been undergoing severe decline as well. By the time that the French king, Louis VI, decided to make it his royal residence (moving there in the early 1100s from the comparative comforts of Orléans), little remained of the town that had prospered under the Romans and the early Merovingians. Centuries of Viking raids and bloody infighting had done their worst, and when Louis looked around, he saw a tiny islanded town surrounded by hostile warlords. Chief among these was Robert of Beaumont, lord of Monceau-Saint-Gervais, who as count of Meulan and earl of Leicester had emerged as one of the most powerful hench-men of the English king.

Paris was thus unquestionably unfriendly, but Louis decided to risk settling there. He carefully fortified his palace (on the western end of the Ile de la Cité) against Anglo-Norman attack as well as against the likes of Robert of Beaumont, who was perfectly capable of crossing to the Cité to create havoc. As he did, after some of the young hotheads in Louis' entourage decided to attack Robert's castle in Meulan. Robert's retaliatory raid on the Cité gave Louis considerable incentive to rethink his island defenses as well as his strategy for subduing the neighbors.

His new strategy involved a long and careful process, carried out with infinite patience, firmness, and attention to detail. He began by replacing the wooden bridge connecting the Cité to the Right Bank (the only Right Bank access to the island) with a great six-arched stone bridge. He then erected a massively fortified tower gate, the Châtelet, at the bridge's entrance. By the end of this determined monarch's long reign (in 1137), he had piece-by-piece secured Paris and its immediate environs.

So much so that by the time Robert of Beaumont's twin sons reached adulthood, they were careful not to offend the increasingly commanding French monarchs in their back yard. By the late twelfth century, when Richard Lionheart faced off against the young French king, Philip Augustus, Robert of Beaumont's grandson would find himself forced to choose between his French and English overlords.

Still, as Paris prospered and grew, the chateau and village of Monceau remained sufficiently outside the ever-more-encompassing series of city walls that it was able to go its own way. No wonder Jeanne d'Arc felt safe resting here en route to besieging the walls of Paris, during the interminable madness of the Hundred Years' War.

Monceau's chateau disappeared long ago, but its memory lingers in the nearby Parc Monceau (8th), a jewel-like garden of winding paths, specimen trees, and shimmering flowers. Here, where the Beaumonts once held sway, mothers and nannies walk their children, and elderly dowagers softly gossip. Yet even today's pristine lawns and gentle hillocks whisper of a turbulent past. The park itself is the legacy of Philippe, Duke of Orléans, who capped a life of dissolution by shrewdly reinventing himself as Philippe-Egalité, a revolutionary champion of the common man. Scarcely a year after casting his vote for Louis XVI's execution, politically ambitious Egalité followed his king to the guillotine—but not before carving out a garden of enchantment at Monceau.

The current park is in fact only a portion of Philippe-Egalité's original retreat; the rest has become one of Paris' most elegant quarters. Yet the colonnaded pool and ancient bowers

Rotonde de Chartres, Parc Monceau

remain, as does the rotunda that still graces Monceau's northern entrance. Ironically, this is the same rotunda that in Egalité's day housed a team of hated tax collectors, who originally set Paris on the path to Revolution.

Today, there is not a tax collector in sight, and it has been centuries since the Beaumonts rode roughshod over these lands. But as you dream your afternoon away among Monceau's flowers, don't let today's tranquil setting deceive you. Monceau is a lady with a past.

V

WALLS and WARS

II.

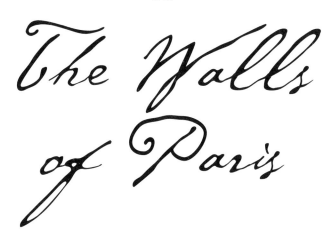

The Walls of Paris

IT MAY SEEM ODD, BUT NOT ALL THAT MANY YEARS AGO, Paris did indeed have walls—real, working walls, meant to keep out an enemy. And although it may seem strange to think of the City of Light enveloped by bristling defenses, this has been exactly the case for much of its history.

In fact, Paris has had many walls, each encircling the city like so many rings on a tree. Just as rings tell the story of a tree's growth, these walls tell the story of a city's growth. For Paris' walls, or series of walls, have given the city its distinctive shape—not only the outwardly spiraling outline of its arrondissements, but the arch of its Grands Boulevards, the curvature of its No. 2 and No. 6 Métro lines (circling Paris from the Arc de Triomphe to the Place de la Nation), and the familiar path of its beltway, the Périphérique.

The earliest of this long string of fortifications dates from almost two millennia ago, the third century AD, when the

Romans forged a stout set of defenses to protect Gallo-Roman Paris (Lutetia) from barbarian attacks. Erecting sturdy walls around the Ile de la Cité as well as their nearby forum, the Romans turned the entire town into a military outpost.

Nothing remains above ground of the forum or its defensive walls, which encompassed the entire Left Bank area from Rue Soufflot to Rue Cujas, between Rue Saint-Jacques and Boulevard Saint-Michel (5th). But a visit to the Crypte Archéologique, beneath the Place du Parvis that fronts Notre-Dame, brings you face-to-face with the remains of the third-century Gallo-Roman wall that once encircled the Ile de la Cité. (Remember that the Cité was a far smaller and lower place two millennia ago, before Seine silt and human landfill did their work.) You can find another trace of Roman wall at 6 Rue de la Colombe, on the Cité's northern side.

Centuries after the Romans, when Paris was struggling with yet another onslaught—this time from the Norse—Eudes, Count of Paris, built a wooden precursor to Louis VI's Châtelet at the entrance to the wooden bridge linking the Right Bank to the Ile de la Cité. (Eudes wisely built a similar defense on the Left Bank as well.) Not only did this Châtelet and its stone successor protect the Cité, but by the twelfth century it anchored a wooden stockade that some historians believe encircled a portion of the Right Bank, which by then was emerging as the city's commercial quarter.

Nothing remains of this stockade, of course, although you can find hints of its former presence. Its eastern gate, Porte Baudoyer, bestowed its name on Place Baudoyer (4th). Winding its way across the quarter, Rue François-Miron follows the path of an ancient road that entered the stockade through Porte Baudoyer, linking Paris to the east.

Wooden defenses and the crumbling remains of Roman walls seemed to have done the job for a while, but by the late twelfth century a new threat—this time from the King of England—set the French to building a far sturdier set of fortifications. Philip II (later called Philip Augustus) responded vigorously to the fact that the English monarch (the famed Richard the Lionheart) was also duke of Normandy and half of France besides. Philip surrounded Paris with stone ramparts 10 feet wide and 30 feet high, punctuated by a battery of towers and reinforced with a deep ditch. He also erected a formidable riverside castle, the Louvre, to the immediate west of these fortifications, providing extra muscle in the direction from which the enemy was expected to attack.

Neither Lionheart nor his immediate successors put Philip's for-

Philip Augustus Wall, Rue Clovis

tifications to the test, but you can still see this fortress' massive foundations, recently excavated and now dramatically displayed beneath the Louvre's Cour Carrée.

You can also find fragments of Philip's eight hundred-year-old wall. The best known of these are the section near the Panthéon (Rue Clovis at Rue du Cardinal-Lemoine, 5th) and the impressive tower-to-tower stretch along Rue des Jardins-Saint-Paul (4th).

There are other lesser-known remnants of this ancient fortification, some of which turn up in surprising places. On the Right Bank, for example, take a look at the stunning fifteenth-century Tour Jean-sans-Peur (now open to the public at 20 Rue Etienne-Marcel, 2nd), which incorporates a portion of Philip's wall, including the base of one of its many towers. On nearby Rue des Francs-Bourgeois (4th), Crédit Municipal's inner courtyard contains a splendid tower base (with newer top) plus an outline of the diagonal course the wall took through these parts, en route to the river.

On the Left Bank, at 4 Cour du Commerce Saint-André (6th), the Catalonian tourist office has preserved a magnificent three-story tower from Philip's wall, incorporating it into a chic renovation. Closer to the river, at 27 Rue Mazarine (adjoining Passage Dauphine, 6th), you will find a beautifully restored wall section plus a tower base on the first and second subterranean levels of a parking garage.

Once you get the hang of it, you'll know where to look. Philip repeated his monumental towers every sixty meters along the wall, which extended from the Louvre and a matching Left Bank tower on the west to the Rue des Jardins-Saint-

Paul segment and its Left Bank counterpart to the east. The Tour Jean-sans-Peur portion stands close to the wall's northernmost point, while the piece near the Panthéon is about as far south as the fortifications got before curving back toward the river (the Place de la Contrescarpe, 5th, marked the southern point of the counterscarp, or sloping outer side of the ditch surrounding the wall). Also remember that any nearby street incorporating the word *fossé* (moat or ditch) in its name is a good clue to follow. Rue Mazarine, by the way, was once called Rue des Fossés-de-Nesle, while Rue Monsieur-le-Prince was once Rue des Fossés-Monsieur-le-Prince.

Having completed his massive fortification, Philip is said to have embraced his architect and announced, "There is now a king, and a France." Unquestionably Paris was now far more secure, and it was not until almost two centuries later, after major hostilities once again broke out between France and England, that a French king decided to update his capital's defenses.

By this time (the late fourteenth century), the burgeoning city had grown into a cramped metropolis that was pushing hard against the confines of Philip's outdated wall. Given England's crushing victories on French soil, France's king Charles V determined to do something about the antiquated ramparts that so indifferently defended—and so grievously constrained—his people.

His solution was to build a new wall, encircling a far larger area. But unlike Philip, he chose to place this bristling new fortification around only the commercial Right Bank, which by this time had far outstripped the university-centered Left Bank

in growth and prosperity. Leaving the Left Bank to whatever
protection Philip's ramparts could still provide, Charles flung
his bulwarks in a wide arc from approximately the site of the
present Place du Carrousel (in the midst of today's Louvre) in
the west to his formidable new fortress, the Bastille, in the east.

Moving the old city gates outward along such major thor-
oughfares as Rue Saint-Denis and Rue Saint-Martin to the
north, and Rue Saint-Antoine and Rue Saint-Honoré to the
east and west, he in effect created a new and larger shell for the
prospering Right Bank city within. He also provided protection
for the new royal palace at the Hôtel Saint-Paul (the site now
bounded by Rue Saint-Paul, Rue Saint-Antoine and Rue du
Petit-Musc in the 4th, near the Bastille) and the Louvre, which
he now converted into a royal residence.

Some two centuries later, as religious and civil warfare
engulfed France, yet another Charles (Charles IX) and a
Louis (Louis XIII) extended this wall in an arc from the
Saint-Denis gate westward, to encompass the city's growing
Right Bank. The wall now stretched from the Bastille in the
east to a point ending between the present-day Place de la
Concorde and the Tuileries in the west.

Remnants of this wall unexpectedly came to light during
recent renovations of the Musée de l'Orangerie (Place de la
Concorde, 1st), where a lengthy section has now been preserved. You can also find vestiges of the Bastille's counterscarp
(in the Bastille station of the No. 5 Métro line) as well as the
site of Charles V's Saint-Honoré gate, marked by a bas-relief
of Jeanne d'Arc's head (161-163 Rue Saint-Honoré, 1st).

Most importantly, though, you can still trace the course of Louis XIII's wall as you stroll down the Grands Boulevards, from the Place de la Madeleine (8th) in the west all the way to the Place de la Bastille in the east, for the Sun King himself, Louis XIV, laid out these most Parisian of all promenades along the course of his father's defensive wall, which he pulled down in the wake of satisfying victories over all his enemies. The word "boulevard" itself, historians remind us, derives from an old German word for "bulwark."

Louis XIV, who never did things by halves, also demolished the old fortified entry gates of Saint-Martin and Saint-Denis, erecting in their place the triumphal arches that still remain (bordering the 10th). These arches framed ceremonial entries into the city until the nineteenth century, when the Arc de Triomphe took their place.

Until the Sun King sent out his demolition crews, the successive walls of Paris had served for centuries to keep out danger, whether enemy troops or—as in the case of the Hôpital Saint-Louis, built just outside city walls—the plague. (Now a greatly expanded full-time hospital, Hôpital Saint-Louis still retains its seventeenth-century core, at 2 Place du Docteur-Alfred-Fournier, 10th.)

But since Philip's time, the walls of Paris had also served the king in quite another capacity—that of foiling smugglers intent on evading the traditionally steep royal tariffs on incoming goods. The disappearance of Louis XIII's wall left the royal tax collectors in the lurch, giving resourceful Parisians a major assist in bypassing the tollgates.

The royal solution was simple and dramatic: a new wall around Paris, this time one whose sole purpose was to buttress the royal tax collectors, or tax farmers, called the Farmers General. This wall, known as the Farmers General wall, went up in a hurry in the 1780s, ringing Paris with more than fifty toll-houses linked by a wall 10 feet high and more than 15 miles in circumference. Much of Paris' population was devastated by this turn of events, which sent prices soaring.

Oddly, those responsible for the wall seemed to think that Parisians would find their new constraint more acceptable— even a matter of pride—if it appeared to be a magnificent work of art, a kind of "garland" around Paris. They could not have been more mistaken. Instead, the very grandness of the numerous neoclassical tollhouses designed by Claude-Nicolas Ledoux, one of the foremost architects of his day, stirred up an extraordinary degree of anger and resentment. Even aficionados of neoclassical architecture, such as Thomas Jefferson (who served as American minister to France during the 1780s), heartily despised them. Not surprisingly, the people of Paris destroyed many of these hated "temples of commerce" during the opening clashes of the Revolution.

Only four of these controversial tollhouses have survived. On the Left Bank, twin buildings—the remains of the old tollgate, the Barrière d'Enfer—still stand at Place Denfert-Rochereau (14th), where one now serves as an entrance to the Catacombs. On the Right Bank, a small rotunda (capped by a nineteenth-century dome) graces the northern entrance to Parc Monceau (8th), marking what once was the Monceau toll barrier. Far to the east, in the Place de la Nation (11th and 12th), two columns dramatically mark the old Barrière du Trône tollgate. (The statues that top these columns, added later, are of Philip Augustus and St. Louis.) Twin buildings flanking these columns once served as offices and lodgings.

Most striking by far is the Rotonde de la Villette (19th), at the foot of the Bassin de la Villette by Place de la Bataille-de-Stalingrad. The largest of the surviving tollhouses, and the centerpiece of the misjudged "garland" that Ledoux cast around Paris, this massive rotunda (based on Palladio's Villa Rotonda) guarded a convergence of northern routes into Paris, including the old Roman road to the sea. A strange relic of the *Ancien Régime* in this working-class neighborhood, the rotunda—set in a pleasant park—survives the indignities of the nearby Métro (which here streams past above ground), just as it somehow managed to survive the revolutionary mobs two centuries ago.

The Farmers General wall itself managed to survive for many years, owing to the fact that Napoléon Bonaparte and subsequent regimes found both it—and the income it collected— useful. In 1860 the government at last took it down, leaving only the boulevards that had run beside it and, eventually, the No. 2 and No. 6 Métro lines to mark its course.

By this time Paris had continued its surge outward into areas such as Passy, Montmartre, and Belleville. Reflecting this new ring of growth, the government had already enclosed Paris within yet a larger and more bristling wall. Named after its then-premier, Adolphe Thiers, the Thiers Fortifications (1841–45) eventually marked Baron Haussmann's administrative limits for Paris, complete with the arrondissements as they exist today. In time, the Thiers wall also replaced the Farmers General wall as a tax barrier. But from the outset its chief function was defensive, reflecting concern for Paris' security in the post-Napoleonic world.

The enemy no longer was England but Prussia and a reunited Germany. Yet the Thiers fortifications did little to stop the Germans during the 1870 Franco-Prussian War, and never saw action during World War I. One of the first things the French did to inaugurate the peace in 1919 was to pull down these outdated ramparts.

Originally, in addition to the unlamented wall, the Thiers fortifications included sixteen forts built outside the wall's perimeter. Despite heavy bombardment and destruction during the Franco-Prussian War and the subsequent Commune uprising, many of these forts still survive and now serve as nuclei for more modern military installations.

Little else of the Thiers fortifications now remains except for the names of its many gates. But you can easily trace the wall's general course by driving the Périphérique. Defining Paris' current city limits (with the exception of the adjacent Bois de Boulogne and Bois de Vincennes), the Périphérique provides yet another shell around a city that has outgrown and cast off a remarkable series of ever-larger shells.

The next time you inch your way through bumper-to-bumper Périphérique traffic, remember that you are also following—albeit slowly—the latest in a succession of rings marking two grand millennia of growth for this remarkable city.

12.

The Maid of Orléans

EARLY ONE MORNING IN SEPTEMBER 1429, THE already-legendary Jeanne d'Arc trained her army's cannon on the walls of Paris. This singular event took place during the height of the Hundred Years' War, a wretched contest between France and England that had already dragged on for years. Actual pitched battles such as Poitiers and Agincourt, although blood-soaked, were few and far between. The real devastation came from bands of rapacious and unemployed mercenaries, who fed and amused themselves between jobs by ravaging the French countryside.

Few among the suffering French peasants could have cared much about the conflict's origins, a territorial contest fueled by England's claim to the French throne. Quite naturally, the French monarch took issue, and war ensued—complicated by a major power struggle in France, in which one of the parties, the powerful House of Burgundy, made common cause with the English. With the invaluable assistance of the Burgundians,

England's young Henry V followed up his victory at Agincourt with a deal that wed him to the French princess and established him (rather than the French dauphin, Charles) as heir to the French throne. But within two years the young hero was dead, leaving a nine-month-old infant in his place.

It was a perfect time for a French hero to emerge. Jeanne d'Arc, the devout daughter of French peasants, responded to the call, obeying heavenly voices that urged her to go to the aid of the dispossessed French dauphin. Overcoming all obstacles through her utter conviction in the divine origin of her mission, she proved a surprisingly able soldier as well as a startlingly charismatic leader.

Under her leadership, a French army succeeded in raising the siege of Orléans (thus earning her the sobriquet, the Maid of Orléans). Even more astonishingly, she persuaded the timid Charles to claim the crown, and accompanied him to Reims for his coronation as Charles VII—a major turning point in the war. Soon after, she led an army to besiege Paris, which was then in the hands of the Burgundians and the English. It seemed obvious to her that the French had to clear the English out of the royal capital before booting them entirely out of France.

Unfortunately Charles was surrounded by advisers who distrusted Jeanne's abilities and envied her influence with him. Working to undermine her, they persuaded the king not to sanction her siege of Paris. Frantic at this abandonment, Jeanne sent plea after plea to Charles while ordering search parties to reconnoiter Paris' walls.

These massive fourteenth-century ramparts, a recent addition to the city's fortifications, protected the bustling commercial area of the Right Bank in a semicircle stretching from the Louvre to the Bastille. High and thick, these walls rose behind a broad and deep moat fed by the Seine. Jeanne had previously encountered city walls, most notably at Orléans, but she had never before encountered anything of this magnitude.

At last, with Charles' tepid support, she made her decision for the assault, lining up her cannon on the Butte Saint-Roch outside the Saint-Honoré Gate, on the city's western flank. Neither the gate nor the hill remain—the Saint-Honoré Gate was demolished after newer walls superseded it, while Baron Haussmann later leveled the Butte Saint-Roch to create the sweeping Avenue de l'Opéra. But you can locate the gate's site, at 161–163 Rue Saint-Honoré (Place André-Malraux, between the Louvre and the Palais Royal, 1st), marked by a bas-relief of the Maid's head. Nearby, in the Place des Pyramides, Frémiet's heroic golden statue pays more flamboyant tribute.

While the king dithered, Jeanne prayed—an all-night vigil at the thirteenth-century chapel of Saint-Denys de la Chapelle (16 Rue de la Chapelle, 18th). This Romanesque chapel still remains, adjoining a modern church dedicated to Sainte-Jeanne d'Arc. An armed statue of her stands guard just outside the door.

After receiving Communion, the Maid departed, leading her troops toward the Saint-Honoré Gate, which was well fortified by towers and deeply moated. Experienced now in war, Jeanne knew that her men would first have to fill the moat with sticks and straw before even attempting to take the structure. So she fearlessly did what she would ask of her own men, testing the moat's depth with her lance.

A deadly crossbow bolt zinged out from above, piercing her thigh. Her men carried her to a nearby refuge to treat her wound, and then—over her protestations—brought her back to the safety of Saint-Denys de la Chapelle. The next morning, despite severe pain, she insisted on leading the attack.

Charles now washed his hands of the entire operation. Despite the Maid's protests, there was little she could do but withdraw. Now marked by failure, she was

Jeanne d'Arc,
Saint-Denys de la Chapelle

relegated to the war's fringes and then captured. Charles failed to intervene on her behalf, and she died at the stake—convicted of witchcraft—in 1431.

The inspiration she provided did not die with her. Within two decades France achieved its long-sought victory, ousting the English from all but a toehold in Calais. More than five centuries later, the Maid of Orléans lives on—as a saint, as a symbol for French nationalism, and as a vivid historic figure who still captures our imaginations.

13.

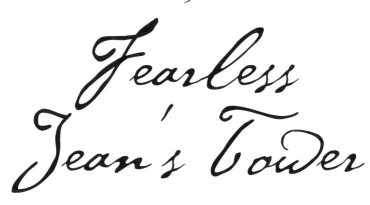

Fearless Jean's Tower

"IT WAS A RUIN WHEN I FIRST SAW IT," SAYS BENOÎTE Taffin, Mayor of Paris' 2nd arrondissement. "But the first time I stepped inside I sensed the magic."

It is that sense of magic, a certain presence of the past, that has at long last brought back to life the ancient Tour Jean-sans-Peur (20 Rue Etienne-Marcel, 2nd). Captivated by the tower's innate grandeur, as well as by its vivid history, private citizens have joined with public sources of funding in an unusual joint venture to save this long-forgotten landmark.

The results are impressive. According to legend, Jean-sans-Peur, Duc de Bourgogne (Burgundy), originally built the tower (1409–11) as a place of refuge following his assassination of Louis d'Orléans, brother of the king. But it is more likely that the fearless duke erected it as a highly visible and impressive symbol of his power. After all, civil war between the Burgundians and the House of Orléans had erupted following the assassination, and the duke had just returned to Paris in triumph after defeating supporters of the House of Orléans. This left Jean-sans-Peur and his followers well in charge of Paris.

What a showpiece he built! Soaring high above his Parisian quarters at the now-defunct Hôtel de Bourgogne, and muscled right up against the twelfth-century city wall, Duke Jean's tower bristled with rugged stonework. Its spiral staircase and open stories effectively islanded its topmost floors, where legend tells us that Jean hid out.

Ironically, this formidable tower never had to prove its military worth, for Jean's enemies never dared attack him inside Paris. Instead, in a perfectly executed act of vengeance, they assassinated him outside the city. After that, the tower fell into decline until the nineteenth century, when enthusiasts rediscovered its romantic ruins. Although they managed to have it classified as an historic monument, they did little to save it until the 1990s. Even then, interest at first was limited to shoring up the dangerously deteriorating structure.

Yet the tower's plight had already attracted the attention of Rémi Rivière, a trained archeologist who grew up in the 2nd arrondissement and had always loved the neglected structure. Deciding to open it to the public, he spent several years researching and developing exhibits to give visitors historical context as well as glimpses into fifteenth-century daily life.

He also ventured into what was for Parisians very new fund-raising territory by creating the Association des Amis de la Tour Jean-sans-Peur (Friends of the Tower of Jean-sans-Peur), to provide ongoing private financial support. Although Madame Taffin and the Ville de Paris freed up substantial public funding for the project, it was this pioneering effort of using private funds to fill the remaining gap that ultimately turned a dream into reality.

When the tower at last opened to the public in October 1999, its many supporters celebrated the long-awaited event with understandable pride. The Tour Jean-sans-Peur is the only medieval fortified structure in Paris to have survived intact, and it is a beauty. Its spiral staircase is dramatic, and its carved vaulting (entwined branches and leaves of oak, hawthorn, and hop vine) is unequaled in France. Without half trying, the tower captures the imagination and draws the visitor back into another world.

But it is a world that is expensive to maintain. Now that the tower is open to the public, it relies entirely upon admission fees and private support to keep it going. Intensifying this challenge is a delicate relationship with the next-door school, which has prevented the tower from opening its doors to the public during most weekday hours.

This in turn has encouraged Rémi Rivière and the tower's supporters to think creatively about other sources of income, including the idea of renting out the ground floor reception area and tower room for parties and candlelight dinners. This kind of innovative thinking pleases some, but comes as a shock to others, who object to what they view as the commercialization of a private museum.

It's a tough situation, but as the Tour Jean-Sans-Peur enters its seventh century, its many staunch supporters have achieved the difficult task of bringing this landmark back to life. Now they face the equally challenging task of keeping its doors open to the public—a challenge that has only just begun.

Tour Jean-sans-Peur

VI

ROYAL AFFAIRS

14.

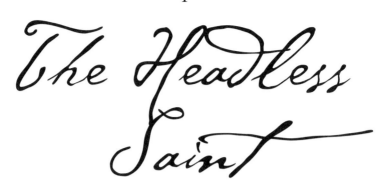

The Headless Saint

THE NEXT TIME YOU'RE IN PARIS AND ARE STANDING in front of Notre-Dame, look closely at its left-hand portal. There, among the freshly cleaned sculptures surrounding this doorway, is a curious one of a saint, complete with halo, holding his head. If you are well-versed in French history, you may recognize him as St. Denis, the first bishop of Paris; but you may not realize the close ties he represents between Notre-Dame and the nearby basilica of Saint-Denis—one of the most remarkable churches ever built.

The origins of these ties lie deep in history, and even deeper in legend, for St. Denis met his death in Paris around the year 273, almost two millennia ago. The Romans, who then occupied Paris, already had their hands full in fighting off barbarian hordes when this charismatic Christian arrived on the scene. According to legend, Roman soldiers tortured Denis near the present site of Notre-Dame and then decapitated him on the slopes of Montmartre.

But this was not the end of the story. According to legend, the martyred saint proceeded to astonish one and all by picking up his head and walking north-ward until he at last col-lapsed on the site now marked by the remarkable basilica (recently desig-nated a cathedral) that bears his name.

As the Empire crum-bled and Roman influ-ence waned, an abbey dedicated to the memory

St. Denis on Notre-Dame

of St. Denis grew up on the place where he so dramatically died. Here, in the eighth century, an abbot of distant mem-ory built a church so fine that Pope Stephen II consecrated Pepin the Short there, securely establishing him on the Frankish throne and paving the way for Pepin's far larger and even more ambitious son, Charlemagne.

Four centuries later, when the visionary Abbot Suger took charge of Saint-Denis, the abbey had acquired a unique and powerful place in the affairs of Paris as well as all of France. Royalty had been buried here ever since King Dagobert, making this church the royal mausoleum. Fairs held under the abbey's auspices had grown to such importance that they bolstered the economy of the entire region. King Louis VI not only deposited the coronation regalia here, but carried into battle the oriflamme, the military standard of the nearby lands over which the abbey held sway. For nearly three centuries thereafter, the French would go into battle bellowing their famous war cry, "Monjoie Saint-Denis!" and carrying before them this flame-colored banner, which became the royal standard of France— even as St. Denis was emerging as the national saint.

What the saint himself would have made of all this is anyone's guess. But Abbot Suger was quite certain of where he stood, in both earthly and heavenly affairs. Observing royal processions entering Paris via the road that linked Saint-Denis to Notre-Dame, and keeping a thoughtful eye on royal funerals making the reverse trip from Notre-Dame to Saint-Denis, he concluded that a new church worthy of the saint's eminent standing should replace the crumbling eighth-century edifice.

The outcome made history. Suger's new church, with its arched and pointed vaults and astonishing deep-blue windows (so blue, in fact, that many believed the glassmaker had infused his molten glass with sapphires) led the twelfth century into those soaring Gothic realms where Chartres, Notre-Dame de Paris, and countless others would soon follow.

Curiously enough, the exterior of Suger's church gives barely a hint of the glories that lie within. But once you get past the single-towered west front (the other tower has long since collapsed), be prepared for an extraordinary experience. The interior of Saint-Denis simply shimmers with light.

Suger was responsible for the west end, including its large round window, which set the stage for all the rose windows to come. He also rebuilt the east end, with its apse and choir, leaving the central section in place until the following century, when this magnificent church once again made architectural history, glorifying God with transepts pierced by near-miraculous rose windows that still glow softly over the tombs of the kings and queens of France.

Look around in the transepts and around the choir, as well as in the crypt. An ancient-looking replica of the oriflamme hides in a shadowy corner on the south side of the ambulatory. Tombs of long-dead monarchs lie everywhere. I'm particularly taken with the tombs of ancient royalty of the sixth and seventh centuries, such as Dagobert, Childebert I, and Frédégonde, wife of Chilperic I. Unfortunately little but their tombs remain—at least in identifiable form. Moved by antimonarchical spirit, the Revolutionaries of the 1790s tore up most of the bodies and threw the bones into a common pit. The tombs still are there, though, and are well worth a look—especially those that date back to the twelfth and thirteenth centuries (ancient replacements for the originals). The eleventh-century mosaic marking the final resting place of Frédégonde is a particular treasure, as is the twelfth-century effigy of Childebert I, the oldest surviving funeral effigy in northern France.

Downstairs, in the crypt, keep an eye out for the ossuary containing the bones that were desecrated by the above-mentioned Revolutionaries. Of particular interest are the excavations, revealing even more ancient tombs as well as the foundations of earlier churches, dating back to the fourth century. Here is the true heart of the basilica, reaching back through the ages. And here, if anywhere, lie the actual remains of the saint who so patiently holds his head alongside the portal of Notre-Dame.

15.

Town and Crown

Perhaps you've seen the Paris version of the "swoosh"—a couple of voluptuously sweeping lines that, with a little imagination, evoke the image of a boat under full sail. It's everywhere, from trash cans to official markers—wherever the city of Paris wishes to place its official insignia. This streamlined logo is a direct descendent of Paris' coat of arms, a far more elaborate and formal affair, with roots going back to the thirteenth century.

It all started with the *marchands de l'eau*, or water merchants, of Paris. Despite their name, these sturdy souls did not lug cases of bottled water into medieval Paris. Instead, they were river boatmen, a guild of men who plied the Seine in a long tradition that went back to Roman times.

But by the thirteenth century, these boatmen no longer were simple working men. Indeed, they had become wealthy and powerful through a series of acquired privileges that allowed them to establish a virtual stranglehold over all goods coming into Paris by water (while the king slapped taxes on whatever came in by land).

The outcome could hardly have been happy for the people of Paris, who as a consequence had to pay far more steeply for the privilege of eating. But it undoubtedly cheered the now-wealthy water merchants as well as their king, who found these tradesmen a splendid source of revenue for all sorts of expensive municipal projects, from street paving to erecting a new set of city walls. In return, the water merchants took an increasingly important role in running the city. In the process, their guild's coat of arms, featuring a small boat, emerged as a permanent feature of Paris' own coat of arms.

The oldest surviving example of this boat insignia is on a seal of the Paris water merchants appended to an accord with the watermen of Rouen. This document, preserved at the Archives Nationales, dates from the year 1210—eight centuries ago.

Following the bloody and almost-successful revolt by Paris' municipal government under Etienne Marcel in 1358, during the darkest days of the Hundred Years War, French monarchs learned to rein in Paris' troublesome governing body. Correspondingly, they also placed their own stamp on the city's evolving coat of arms. Following Marcel's revolt, the dauphin—who was to become Charles V—emphatically placed a section of decidedly royal fleurs-de-lis over the boat, at the top of the escutcheon, or shield.

Throughout the years, Paris' coat of arms, or *blason*, has evolved and changed. Under Napoléon, for example, the imperial bee temporarily replaced the royal fleur-de-lis. With the coming of the Second Republic, in 1848, the fleur-de-lis once again temporarily vanished, replaced by stars.

The *blason* took its present form in 1942. As it now graces the Hôtel de Ville, or City Hall of Paris, this *blason* is a brightly colored composition, almost daunting in its complexity. It helps to focus on its center, an updated version of the water merchants' simple boat. This stylized vessel of silver rides on equally stylized silver waves and dominates the heraldic escutcheon, whose background is red—a color intentionally evocative of the city's often-bloody struggles for liberty and independence.

Red is also significant as the color of Saint-Denis—the cathedral where countless generations of French royalty are buried. Saint-Denis provided the oriflamme, the scarlet banner that inspired French armies as they charged into battle, long before the fleur-de-lis came to symbolize French royalty. But by Charles V's day, the fleur-de-lis had become the royal symbol, while blue had become the royal color. Note the band of golden fleurs-de-lis against a background of blue at the escutcheon's top, where Charles V originally placed it.

This escutcheon is wearing a crown—a very peculiar crown, actually, for it has all the markings of a castle, including crenellations along its top, and the outlines of stones across its walls. Symbolism is essential to heraldry, as you have already noticed, and this crown with its five towers symbolizes the ancient city of Paris protected by its ramparts.

Continuing our exploration, we find some greenery curving gently along the escutcheon's sides. To the right is a laurel

Coat of Arms, City of Paris, Hôtel de Ville Métro Station

branch, while to the left is a branch of oak—surely indications of heroism and strength. From the bottom, as if in vindication, hang three medals conferred on the City of Paris within the past century: the Legion of Honor (center), the Cross of War (World War I), and the Cross of Liberation (World War II).

There is a lot going on here, as befits a coat of arms produced over the course of eight centuries. Do not overlook the motto, *Fluctuat nec mergitur*, even though it's in Latin. Roughly translated, it means that Paris, and the boat that symbolizes her, may encounter rough sailing—but she will not sink.

Remember that fighting spirit the next time you encounter the Paris coat of arms, either in its traditional or more modernized forms. Or simply ponder it a bit as you stand on the Pont-Neuf, looking out over the Seine.

16.

A Difficult Queen

MARGUERITE DE VALOIS WAS NO LADY. DAUGHTER OF one king and wife of another, she disported herself in ways considered unseemly by the usually unshockable French court. The scandalmongers lost count of her lovers, although history credits her with at least twenty-three. Her husband, the long-suffering Henri IV (who consoled himself with an even more impressive number of mistresses), at length divorced his adventurous queen and sent her into exile.

Yet after eighteen years (and a second wife), Henri felt a certain remorse. Word had it that Marguerite—now pudgy and bewigged—longed for Paris. What harm could it do to let her return? And so the king installed her in the Hôtel de Sens, a suitably impressive mansion on the Right Bank, along the Seine. Marguerite arrived there in 1605 and immediately set the place swinging. Soon two of her lovers were at each other's throats, and before long one had killed the other at the mansion's door.

Infuriated by the loss of her current favorite, Marguerite did not hesitate. The next day, the luckless survivor went to his own death—on the very doorstep where he had dispatched his rival. Not the fainting kind, Marguerite grimly watched his execution. And then she promptly moved to the Left Bank.

It was, without question, the most newsworthy event ever to come out of the staid Hôtel de Sens. It was rivaled only by Marguerite's memorable encounter with a large fig tree near the front door, which gave offense by blocking her carriage (the tree lost the contest, but the street still is known as the Rue du Figuier). Until Marguerite's arrival, the hôtel had in fact led a most proper existence. Since 1475, when Archbishop Tristan de Salazar began its construction, the hôtel had served as the Paris residence for a series of archbishops of Sens, who claimed the diocese of Paris as an ecclesiastical dependency. Completed in 1519, the Hôtel de Sens became known as one of the most beautiful residences in Paris, concocted in the Flamboyant Gothic style and arrayed with fierce corner turrets—as befitted a feudal dwelling in still-dangerous times.

Tristan de Salazar's successors found less and less reason to be in Paris, and so the mansion remained virtually vacant, an ideal residence for a wayward queen. Fortunately for us, it also remained virtually unchanged, as no one took serious interest in renovating it. But benign neglect turned less benign after 1622, when Paris finally got its own archbishop. Subsequent archbishops of Sens began to rent the place out, and the once-elegant mansion now languished, first as an office for the Lyons stage coach and eventually—reflecting the decline of the entire

Marais district—as a jam factory and glassworks. When the City of Paris came to the building's rescue in 1911, it had a huge renovation job on its hands, but one with a happy ending. Today's Hôtel de Sens (at 1 Rue du Figuier, 4th) is once more a gorgeous feature of Paris' Right Bank, complete with formal French gardens to the rear.

Even if you are not an arts and crafts enthusiast, don't overlook the Bibliothèque Forney upstairs. Here you will find a wealth of reference materials on the decorative arts, including slides, posters, and drawings as well as an impressive array of fabric and wallpaper samples, some dating from the 18th century. If this is not of interest, then browse around the library itself—a magnificent room of carved stone and beamed ceilings. Off to the left, duck into the tower and explore the spiral staircase, which leads to other nooks and corners.

A great destination for a rainy day, the Hôtel de Sens is also remarkable after dark, either with or without a moon (it's almost magical on a misty night). Now one of the oldest surviving examples of domestic architecture in Paris, it effortlessly evokes the beauty and violence of a dangerous queen and a now-distant past.

17.

Royal Mysteries

S HELTERED AGAINST THE NORTH SIDE OF THE OLD
church of Sainte-Marguerite (36 Rue Saint-Bernard, 11th) lies a
small grave with a tiny white cross. Its inscription is brief but
haunting: "L XVII 1785–1795." For here is the final resting
place of the ten-year-old dauphin, Louis XVII.

Or so many have believed. According to legend, on the night
of June 10, 1795, an anonymous yet official-looking funeral procession slowly made its way from the Temple prison to the
graveyard of Sainte-Marguerite, which already held hundreds of
guillotined bodies from the Place de la Bastille. With no ceremony, the officials laid the unmarked coffin in the common pit
and departed. But after they left, the gravedigger—who had his
suspicions—dug up the small coffin, marked it with a fleur-de-
lis, and placed it in a special spot against the church wall.

Thus the legend of the Temple child was born. All knew
that the dauphin, the only surviving son of Louis XVI and

Marie Antoinette, had been imprisoned in the great Temple Tower (originally built by the Knights Templar), along with his sister and parents. Indeed, the king went to the guillotine from there on January 21, 1793, while the queen remained at Temple Tower until August, when she departed for the Conciergerie and death (October 16, 1793). The dauphin stayed on, thrown into solitary confinement, mistreated by his jailers, and reduced to a diseased and pitiful wreck. According to the French Revolutionary government, he died on June 8, 1795—two days before the mysterious funeral procession to Sainte-Marguerite.

But the very secrecy surrounding his death gave rise to rumors that he had escaped—a tantalizing possibility that led to numerous pretenders to the French throne. More than forty would-be candidates eventually emerged, and dubious "lost dauphins" became such a staple of nineteenth-century life that Mark Twain even included a shady "dauphin" among his fictitious riverbank characters in *Huckleberry Finn*.

With the return of monarchy in 1814, Louis XVIII—the elder of Louis XVI's two surviving brothers—took little interest in tracking down the actual fate of the little dauphin (who, if still alive, would have stood between him and the throne). But he did immediately go to work to locate the remains of his brother and sister-in-law, Louis XVI and Marie Antoinette. These lay unmarked in a cemetery just north of the Place de la Concorde (or Place de la Révolution), where the king and queen had died. Like other mass graves that appeared throughout Paris during the height of the Terror, including the

Cimetière de Picpus (12th) and the once-large cemetery of Sainte-Marguerite, this cemetery held the bodies of hundreds of unfortunates brought from the guillotine, as well as the detritus of other disasters.

Much as with the burial of the Temple child, someone took careful note of where the king and queen were buried and marked the exact location. Louis XVIII had the royal bodies exhumed and moved to the basilica of Saint-Denis, joining a long line of defunct French kings and queens. Then he erected an imposing monument on the site—the solemn Chapelle Expiatoire (Square Louis-XVI, Boulevard Haussmann, 8th).

In this way, closure was reached for the unfortunate king and queen, but the lost dauphin's story still remained unfinished. Not until 1846 did anyone examine the mysterious body in the cemetery of Sainte-Marguerite, and when the coffin was opened, those presiding over this delicate operation discovered the body of a young man considerably older than the dauphin's ten years. In 1894 a more scientific inquest reached the same conclusion. Where, then, was the little lost dauphin?

Except for some of the pretenders' most ardent supporters, most agreed that the young boy had died in the Temple Tower. After all, he had been deathly ill and was abysmally treated. Perhaps he was buried near the tower—or perhaps not. No one knew. But in 1810 Napoléon razed the beautiful medieval tower to prevent Royalists from treating it as a shrine. Today, nothing remains of the edifice, and the pond and waterfall that now

The dauphin's tomb

occupy the attractive Square du Temple (3rd) give no feeling for the historic events that once took place there.

Similarly, the cemetery of Sainte-Marguerite has now been replaced by a courtyard garden, with the small tomb and white cross modestly tucked up against the church wall. No one knows exactly who lies buried here, and the tomb remains a mystery.

Some continue to contend that the young dauphin was smuggled, very much alive, out of the Temple Tower and his place taken by another, presumably older boy. But more than two centuries after the little dauphin's disappearance, scientists have conducted DNA tests that have at last disproved this romantic legend. They contend that the young dauphin did indeed die in the Temple Tower, and that a barely preserved heart plus some snippets of hair prove it.

Oddly enough, the heart of the young boy who died on June 8, 1795, in the Temple prison did indeed survive— although given its subsequent adventures, one wonders how. A doctor presiding at the child's autopsy secreted the heart in his handkerchief, carrying it home and enshrining it in an alcohol-filled crystal urn. The doctor's assistant stole it, the assistant's widow eventually returned it, and the alcohol dried up, but there was still enough left of the relic when the monarchy was restored that the doctor could, with presumably great relief, offer it to the new king.

Louis XVIII proved uninterested in acquiring the preserved heart. In a quandary, the doctor entrusted it to the Archbishop of Paris, who safely kept it until the 1830 uprisings, when a mob stormed his palace. A quick-thinking Royalist made off with the relic, but as he struggled with a national guardsman, the crystal container shattered. Later, the distraught Royalist returned and found the heart lying among the broken glass.

The well-traveled heart now went to the son of the doctor who first pinched it, who in turn passed it along to members of one of the branches of the royal family. Here it quietly remained until 1975, when it joined the rest of the royal family in the crypt at Saint-Denis.

But its adventures were not entirely over. In late 1999, careful hands placed tiny slices of the preserved organ in sealed envelopes and sent them for independent analysis to two laboratories in Germany and Belgium. There, scientists compared the bits of mummified heart with verified locks of hair from Marie Antoinette and other female relatives (fortunately, eighteenth-century families preserved snippets of hair as readily as we preserve photos). And within several months, the results were in.

The outcome? Astonishing news—at least for many Frenchmen. The boy who died at Temple prison in June 1795 was indeed the little dauphin, the son of the beheaded queen.

A mystery solved, and a big one. But other mysteries still remain. No one knows for sure where the dauphin is buried. And no one at all knows who lies buried beneath that little white cross in the cemetery of Sainte-Marguerite.

NOTE: To visit the grave at l'Eglise Sainte-Marguerite (through a locked door on the left), ask at the church office. While there, take a look at the church, which is old and lovely, with some interesting paintings.

VII

MOVERS and SHAKERS

18.

Henri le Grand

NORMALLY I DON'T RECOMMEND RESTROOMS AS cultural attractions, but the hallway alongside the Samaritaine department store's fifth-floor washrooms is an exception. Here, through huge picture windows, spreads a spectacular bird's-eye view of Saint-Germain l'Auxerrois—the Gothic church that almost put an end to young Henri IV at the outset of his extraordinary career. It's a dramatic curtain raiser to Henri's Paris, for here the bells rang out at midnight of Saint Bartholomew's Day, 1572, signaling the assassins to strike.

Henri had come to Paris to wed the Valois princess, Marguerite. As leader of the French Protestants (or Huguenots), he had, quite naturally, brought a large number of Huguenot leaders with him. The idea was that by wedding the Catholic princess, young Henri (then known as Henri of Navarre) would help end the wars of religion that were wreaking havoc throughout France. But Marguerite's mother, the scheming

Catherine de Medici had other ideas, and Henri's wedding almost became his funeral.

French Protestants died by the thousands as the Massacre of Saint Bartholomew swept the land, but Henri himself escaped. He not only survived, but in time became king—converting to Catholicism en route to coronation. Completely pragmatic, Henri had no problem with this purely political solution to virtual anarchy. Paris, as he so famously remarked, was well worth a Mass.

Paris, in fact, was worth a great deal in Henri's eyes. Whatever he thought of the Valois clan—and it couldn't have been complimentary—he certainly held no grudge against the city where the Valois had so unpleasantly entertained him. Throughout his two-decade reign, from 1589 to 1610, he treated Paris like a much-favored mistress (and, admittedly, he had many). "I make war, I make love, and I build," he once remarked, and having established peace, good government, and prosperity throughout France, he turned his attentions to his capital on the Seine. In this, he had the eye of a city planner, for the vast building program on which he embarked had a coherency that still defines important parts of Paris today.

This is especially true of his vision for the city's gateways. Surrounded by massive fortifications (which would not disappear until the reign of his grandson, Louis XIV), Paris at the outset of Henri's reign lacked a ceremonial entrance that met the new king's standards. First contemplating the city's western approach, Henri thoughtfully considered the Louvre, where

François I had already demolished the old fortress and begun to build. He also gave due attention to the nearby Palais des Tuileries, which his fearsome mother-in-law, Catherine de Medici, had constructed just outside the city walls. Then he cast his eye on the Pont-Neuf, begun under the reign of his predecessor. From these disparate elements Henri created a well-conceived and still-ravishing whole, which provided a breathtaking first view of Paris for those entering from the west.

Key to his plan was an enormous Gallery along the Seine, starting at the Louvre and extending westward to the Tuileries Palace, where it terminated in the Pavillon de Flore. The Palais des Tuileries may no longer exist, but Henri's mammoth undertaking—known as the Louvre's Grande Galerie, or Galerie du Bord de l'Eau (Waterside Gallery)—still astonishes visitors today, just as it did four centuries ago. One admirer in 1599 called it "the greatest and goodliest Palace of Europe." Another, practically gasping for breath, reported that one "can hardly comprehend it in his mind."

Tramping along inside the Gallery, surrounded by acres of pictures, today's footsore visitor may not fully grasp the grandeur of Henri's vision, which is best understood from a quayside perspective. Not only did the vast structure succinctly convey this monarch's power and might, but for four centuries it has led the eye toward the beautiful architectural grouping at the Ile de la Cité's sculpted prow.

Central to this grouping is the Pont-Neuf, the so-called New Bridge that, as everyone knows, is now the oldest bridge in Paris. The Pont-Neuf may have had its birth during the reign of

Henri's predecessor, but in the end owed its existence to Henri himself. It was a remarkable achievement. For more than a thousand years, other bridges had connected the Ile de la Cité with both Right and Left Banks, but these had taken the relatively easy way out. The earliest of these spanned the Seine at its narrowest point, connecting what is now Rue Saint-Jacques with Rue Saint-Martin. Those that followed avoided the western part of the island, where the royal palace and gardens posted a virtual "Keep Out" sign. In addition to preserving royal privacy and security, this bridge-free policy recognized certain realities, from the width of the required northern span to the marshy nature of the island's tip, which drifted into inconsequential and flood-prone islets.

Generally abandoned, these islets proved little more than an eyesore until a bridge here became necessary to relieve congestion on the Ile de la Cité's other spans. Soon this waterlogged area was drained, the islets joined into what is now the much-loved Square du Vert-Galant, and a massive terrace built up to support the central portion of the new bridge—a striking stone structure that Henri IV completed in 1607. As a finishing touch, the king now conveyed grounds between palace and bridge for the Place Dauphine, an innovative open-air square for Paris' bourgeoisie.

Far from holding the powerful middle class at arm's length, Henri—an earthy and engaging man—thought it prudent to provide a centrally located and inviting place for Parisian merchants and bankers to carry out their work. Yet he had no intention of allowing hodge-podge development in this prime location. As with his other building projects around Paris, he stipulated that all structures in the Place Dauphine—named after the Dauphin, or future Louis XIII—adhere to strict uniformity, with matching brick-and-stone houses lined around a shady triangular park. Although Henri's original concept has suffered considerable indignities, including upper additions, altered façades, and the destruction of the entire row of houses along the square's eastern side, the Place Dauphine has managed to retain its beauty, remaining a serene and secluded spot.

Together, all of these architectural elements still work in tandem to give harmonious and elegant definition to the island's western tip. The Pont-Neuf, a particularly graceful span, was never cluttered with shops and houses like the other bridges of Paris. It was wide, it was paved, and—wonder of wonders—it had pedestrian sidewalks, a practical and farsighted first that came complete with artistic benefits, giving this bridge a clean line from the start.

Between the Pont-Neuf's two spans and near original ground level lies the narrow point now named the Square du Vert-Galant, in honor of Henri and his legendary amorous adventures. This quiet spot, a favorite for lovers, is one of the best places in Paris to spend a quiet afternoon—snoozing, reading, or simply watching the boats go by.

Up the stairs and between the two bridge spans you will find the old fellow himself, sculpted in the best equestrian manner. Pause for a moment to consider whether he is facing the right direction (shouldn't he be overlooking the Square du Vert-Galant?), then continue across the Pont-Neuf for a quick look at the Left Bank portion of Henri's original scheme. Here, carving out new cityscapes, he established yet another fashionable set of addresses along Rue Dauphine, Rue Christine (named after one of Henri's daughters), and little Passage Dauphine (a delightful out-of-the way enclave).

But Henri's vision did not stop with the western end of Paris. At the time of his death he was planning a new eastern entry to the city, to replace the cramped Saint-Antoine gateway at the massively fortified Bastille. Instead of rebuilding at the old location, he chose a site near today's Place de la République, where—in a style worthy of Baron Haussmann—he contemplated broad avenues radiating out like spokes, linked by a semicircular boulevard. In all, his planned gateway was to have an impressive number of streets (named after France's regions and provinces), as well as public gardens and a beautiful Seine-fed canal—a vision that anticipated the nearby Canal Saint-Martin by some two centuries.

If you follow the Rue Vieille-du-Temple out past the Musée Picasso, you will soon find yourself in the area that Henri envisioned as his eastern gateway, which he named the Place de France (3rd). Today only a few of the "spokes" of this gateway remain (Rue de Normandie, Rue de Bretagne, and Rue de Poitou), linked by the semicircular Rue Debelleyme. Just beyond, to the east, runs the Boulevard des Filles-du-Calvaire, marking the course of the old city walls. This area's once-elegant seventeenth- and eighteenth-century houses are now in various states of disrepair but evoke a gritty romanticism. Here, among encroaching gentrification, you can still find pockets of a bygone Paris—a shabby but fascinating domain of lamplight and shadows.

For quite the opposite effect, see Henri's Place des Vosges, just to the south. Hugging the border between the 3rd and 4th arrondissements, this breathtaking open-air square exudes elegance, from the Hotel Pavillon de la Reine on the north to the exclusive l'Ambroisie restaurant tucked discreetly into the southwest corner.

In the fifteenth and sixteenth centuries, the royal family occupied a sumptuous residence (the Hôtel des Tournelles) on this site—that is, until a king met his death here in a bizarre accident. None could save him, and the king's widow, Catherine de Medici (yes, *that* Catherine de Medici), was so devastated she had the entire residence razed. That left a large empty space, and once on the throne, Henri IV took notice. Determined to make his mark here, much as he had throughout the rest of town, he set his architects to create a harmonious and symmetrical square rimmed by thirty-six houses and the splendid Pavillon du Roi to the south, with a slightly smaller Pavillon de la Reine to the north. Built of brick and stone, with steep slate roofs, much like those in the Place Dauphine, these arcaded houses—nine to a side—still comprise one of the most elegant settings in Paris.

Inaugurated with the double wedding of young Louis XIII and his sister to Austrian and Spanish royalty, the square—then known as the Place Royale—became the most fashionable address in town. This chic reputation continued even after Louis XIV established Versailles as *the* place to be, although in time the aristocrats moved out and the neighborhood changed. When Victor Hugo lived here in gloomy Gothic splendor in the 1830s and 1840s, the square existed as a kind of island in the midst of a working-class sea. (Hugo's house, now a museum, is located in the southeastern corner.) By this time, it had shed its royalist name and become the Place des Vosges—in honor of the department of the Vosges, which in 1800 stood first in line to pay its taxes to the new Republic.

Now this magnificent square is once again home to wealth and splendor, conveyed—in characteristic Henri IV fashion—with elegant restraint. For the best introduction, enter through the Pavillon du Roi and linger a while beneath the trees. This may be a high-rent district, but all the quiet park benches are free.

Word of the Place des Vosges' charms has been spreading, but few still seem to know about its virtual twin, just north of the Place de la République. Here, with typical concern for his city's well-being, Henri IV built a hospital for plague victims just outside the city walls. Like the Place des Vosges, and much like the Place Dauphine, the Hôpital Saint-Louis consists of a brick-and-stone quadrangle surrounding a tree-filled courtyard. The similarities have prompted speculation that Claude Chastillon, architect of the Place des Vosges, created this as well. You can visit the rarely crowded courtyard on weekdays, entering through the original gate at 2 Place du Docteur-Alfred-Fournier, just off Rue Bichat, 10th.

Beyond the walled complex lie other original buildings, including the chapel and the Pavillon Gabrielle (where Henri is rumored to have frolicked with his favorite mistress, Gabrielle d'Estrées). These could use some sprucing up, but restoration has already begun on the chapel, and may well proceed to other parts of the compound, where today's modern hospital remains largely out-of-view.

Clearly, Henri was a king who cared. In addition to providing several much-needed hospitals, including the Hôpital Saint-Louis, he widened and paved streets, improved the water supply, and even built a care facility for war veterans—long before his grandson founded the Hôtel des Invalides.

With such a record, it's not surprising that Henri enjoyed great popularity among the lower and middle classes, who found him a man to their taste, plainspoken and approachable. "A chicken in every pot every Sunday," he is said to have promised, and did his best to keep his word.

Unfortunately, he was hated as well—by extremists, religious fanatics, and schemers of all sorts. During the course of his reign he had grown accustomed to assassination attempts (there were nineteen in all), but he refused to go about heavily armed in the city he loved, and whose people he trusted. On May 14, 1610, he was stuck in traffic in his carriage when a deranged assassin—a religious fanatic gripped by visions—leaped up and drove his knife deep into Henri's heart. (You can still see the place where it happened, marked by a large marble slab in the center of the street at 11 Rue de la Ferronnerie, 1st).

Paris and all of France deeply and genuinely mourned his death. Henri le Grand, they call him, one of the greatest, and certainly the most beloved, of French kings. A king who dearly loved Paris and adorned her in the most magnificent fashion, with jewels that still enhance the City of Light today.

NOTE: The Samaritaine department store has unexpectedly closed its doors. There is talk of renovation and eventual reopening (in six to seven years!), but many suspect that this beautiful old *grand magasin* may have closed for good.

19.

Little Giant

TUCKED INTO AN INCONSPICUOUS MUSEUM IN THE shadow of Notre-Dame are two small gilded bees, rare survivors of Napoléon Bonaparte's extravagant imperial coronation of 1804. A small-enough memento of a long-ago event, and yet one still capable of creating a thrill of recognition—exactly as Napoléon intended. Mindful of how quickly grand occasions can disappear into history's dustbin, Bonaparte—aided by a battery of designers and planners, as well as by Jacques-Louis David's monumental painting of the event—infused his coronation with the kind of opulence and drama that history would not easily forget. And so, long after decorations such as these gilded bees (Napoléon's imperial insignia) disappeared from the coronation site at Notre-Dame, the legend lingered on.

Napoléon was not about to leave his place in history to chance. Given his deep and abiding determination to conquer history as well as Europe, this meant staging events such as his coronation with an eye to posterity. It also meant leaving permanent legacies of his event-filled reign, whether by massively overhauling the French legal, financial, and administrative systems, or by gargantuan efforts to build and repair the nation's bridges, harbors, and roads. Intent on reminding countless future generations of his heroism and greatness, he created enduring monuments of the sort no one can ignore. Victories on the battlefield earn one a place in the history books, but Napoléon wanted something more—the kind of instant recognition and acknowledgment accorded to only a very few throughout the centuries.

All of France was his palette, but Paris was his masterpiece, the jewel in his crown. "I intend to make Paris the most beautiful capital in the world," he once remarked, and he set about this task with dizzying focus and energy. He thought in terms of monuments, but he also thought in terms of Paris as a whole—a city that had once glowed with splendor but had suffered widespread destruction during the Revolution. As always, Napoléon's grand vision was based on sound engineering as well as on what he had seen and read of classical Greece and Rome. The outcome, just as he intended, was magnificent.

It is difficult to walk about in the heart of today's Paris without seeing the tangible results of Bonaparte's vision—a vision that so often was inextricably linked with his military victories. The Louvre's Cour Napoléon, for example, recalls the enormous impact he made on this venerable institution. Aided by sharp-eyed experts who took the best from conquered lands, Bonaparte came close to making the Louvre the repository for all of Europe's greatest masterpieces, not to mention a remark-able haul from Egypt. The plunder was incredible, and soon it became clear that more space was needed. Renaming it the Musée Napoléon, Napoléon soon began to make his mark on the building's physical edifice as well.

Work on the Louvre had halted more than a century before, when Louis XIV left for Versailles. Now Napoléon took up the long-standing royal tradition of expanding the complex, under-taking the daunting task of completing its northernmost side all the way to the Tuileries Palace, via a vast connecting gallery. He got about halfway before events intervened. Several decades later, his nephew, Napoléon III, completed the job.

Following Waterloo, his victorious foes wanted their art back, and much of this vast hoard found its way home. (For the record, the Mona Lisa is not one of Napoléon's trophies. She arrived in France with Leonardo and has stayed there ever since, except for a brief hiatus when an Italian workman, mis-takenly thinking that Napoléon was responsible for her Lou-vre residence, attempted to return her to Italy.) Today's Louvre is of course an extraordinary museum, but it is not quite what Napoléon had in mind.

Just beyond the Cour Napoléon rises Bonaparte's famous Arc de Triomphe du Carrousel, built to celebrate some of the emperor's most stunning victories. Modeled after the Arch of Septimus Severus in Rome, this arch originally served as a grand entrance to Napoléon's imperial residence, the Tuileries palace, which then stretched across the western edge of the Louvre complex. (That was before the Communards torched the palace

Arc de Triomphe du Carrousel

in 1871, leaving the Third Republic to raze its charred remains.) Bonaparte topped this fine arch with one of his chief prizes, the four antique horses from St. Mark's, in Venice. These eventually were returned and replaced by a new bronze and gold group starring four similar horses, this time in an arrangement that honored the restored Bourbon monarchy.

The name "Carrousel" considerably predated Bonaparte and his triumphal arch, and in fact summons up memories of Louis XIV, the Sun King. Louis celebrated the birth of his first son by throwing an extravaganza there, featuring an eye-popping equestrian display known as a carrousel. Ever after, this area has been known as the Jardin du Carrousel. Napoléon couldn't erase these associations, but he could and did overwhelm them.

Today, the Jardin du Carrousel and its triumphant arch summon up images of Bonaparte, not Louis XIV.

Napoléon was just as successful in replacing the Sun King in public memory elsewhere in Paris. The Porte Saint-Martin (10th) and neighboring Porte Saint-Denis (10th), which grandly commemorate Louis XIV's military victories, had for more than a century served as the great ceremonial arches into Paris. Napoléon began to build the even more imposing Arc de Triomphe, which in time completely overshadowed Louis' entryways.

Then there is the Invalides (7th). Originally built by the Sun King to house the wounded veterans of his many military campaigns, the Invalides has since 1840 become the single monument most closely associated with Bonaparte, who lies here in imperial splendor. Napoléon fans love it; his critics do not. What Louis would have thought, one can only imagine.

Even before his death, Bonaparte had already placed his mark on this part of town, which he had known longer than any other corner of Paris. As an impoverished fifteen-year-old, he arrived at the famed Ecole Militaire, a still-extant institution founded by Louis XV's notorious mistress, Madame de Pompadour. The second surviving son of a respectable Corsican family with far more in the way of aspirations than property, Napoléon had already established himself as unusually bright, competitive, and something of a loner. After attending the military academy of Brienne, he entered the Ecole Militaire as a scholarship student. There he acquitted himself well, excelling in mathematics and falling in love with history, most especially the history of classical Greece and Rome and the lives of its great men. Short but scrappy, he quickly earned a reputation as studious, curious, arrogant, and proud.

The Ecole Militaire, on Place de Fontenoy, 7th, is not open to visitors, but its beautiful façade (by Jacques-Ange Gabriel) can easily be admired. The view from the adjoining Champ-de-Mars is also impressive. During his year here, Napoléon and his fellow cadets paraded on the Champ-de-Mars. Eventually, of course, he would inspect his own troops here, after a breathtaking rise that made him commander-in-chief of an army by the age of twenty-seven, first consul by the age of thirty, and emperor at thirty-five. In between came victory after victory, with spoils to match. Among the cartloads of money and masterpieces he hauled back from Italy were Venice's other prize, its lion from St. Mark's Square. (After Waterloo, this, too, was returned.)

Napoléon's disastrous retreat from Moscow meant that the Kremlin would keep its treasures, but soon Bonaparte retaliated by laying plans to build a vast imperial city, one that would outshine both the Kremlin and Versailles. Waterloo put an end to this extravagant scheme, intended for the site of the current Place du Tracadéro and Palais de Chaillot (16th), and extending all the way to the Bois de Boulogne.

Also on a grand scale, Bonaparte decided that he would give Paris fountains even more splendid than those of Rome. The large sphinx-bedecked fountain in the Place du Châtelet (1st), commemorating his Egyptian campaigns, is one of these. His heroically proportioned Fontaine de Mars (at the corner of Rue Saint-Dominique and Rue de l'Exposition, 7th), is another.

Of course, to provide a spectacular water display, or even a steady supply of drinking water, required a far better and more reliable water supply than Paris had hitherto enjoyed. Napoléon—thinking on a large scale, as always—began work on an elaborate canal system that would link Paris with the waters of the river Ourcq. Napoléon was not the first to think of this plan. Henri IV had given the idea serious thought, and Louis XIV had also expressed interest. But Napoléon actually put the idea into action, and with remarkable speed. As it happened, he pushed his engineers so hard to complete the work that the end product was less than stable. At the Canal de l'Ourcq's 1808 inauguration ceremony, the canal wall dramatically split open.

Napoléon was not deterred. Within three years, water from the River Ourcq (via the Ourcq canal and new Bassin de la Villette) flowed into the Fontaine du Château-d'Eau—a splendid affair in the midst of what then was known as the Place du Château-d'Eau, but now is called the Place de la République. Time and Baron Haussmann made vast changes here, and now the fountain (also known as the Fontaine aux Lions de Nubie) can be found at the entrance to the Parc de la Villette (19th). Even more changes occurred to the village-like character of the whole area, once the connecting canals of Saint-Martin and Saint-Denis were completed. The canal network fostered a surge of commercial activity and industrialization, and soon the Bassin de la Villette no longer was a place where Parisians came to stroll on a Sunday afternoon. Fortunately today, almost two centuries later, the Canal Saint-Martin and the Bassin de la

Villette are once again emerging as the kinds of pleasure destinations that Bonaparte originally had in mind.

Along with Napoléon's bold network of canals were other
major urban improvements for Paris, including several
bridges: Pont d'Austerlitz (12th), Pont d'Iéna (16th), and the
exquisite Pont des Arts (1st) — a novelty built of iron and limited to pedestrians. Perhaps symbolically, the Pont des Arts
connects the Louvre with the domed building across the
Seine housing the Institut de France (6th). Previously quartered in the Louvre, the Institut moved to its present palatial
premises under Napoléon.

Those who are interested in finance will want to amble over
to Place de la Bourse (2nd), in the heart of what has become
Paris' financial district. Here Napoléon created the Paris stock
exchange, the Bourse, and the imposing neoclassical building
that houses it. Although the building itself was not completed
until after Waterloo, it and the exchange remain an important
legacy of Bonaparte's reign.

It is now time to take a stroll to that section of Paris where
Napoléon made the greatest changes in the city landscape. Not
unexpectedly, it covers ground he knew the best—from the area
around the Ecole Militaire and Invalides on the Left Bank to
the Place Vendôme and the Church of the Madeleine (Sainte-
Marie-Madeleine) on the Right.

Stand on the Right Bank side of the Pont de la Concorde,
and what do you see? Across the river and slightly to the left is
the Hôtel de Salm, much admired by Thomas Jefferson, where
Napoléon placed his famed Legion of Honor. But straight

ahead, where your eye naturally focuses, is the National Assembly. Housed in the former Palais Bourbon, it boasts a neoclassical façade, which replaced the eighteenth-century original.

This was Napoléon's idea, and if you venture onto the bridge and look back, you will see why. Gaze across the Place de la Concorde, all the way to the Madeleine. It's an imposing vista, with the National Assembly's façade matching that of the Madeleine, which Napoléon built in neoclassical style. Despite its ecclesiastical lineage, the Madeleine looks more like a Greek temple—exactly as Bonaparte intended. Declaring it a "Temple of Glory," he dedicated it to his Grand Army. After Waterloo, the Madeleine once again became a church.

Nearby, Napoléon wanted an imposing street leading from the Louvre all the way to the Place de la Bastille. His architects produced the Rue de Rivoli, with its famous arcades. He also insisted on a fine street (Rue de Castiglione) connecting the Rue de Rivoli with the Place Vendôme. But it was the street connecting Place Vendôme with today's Place de l'Opéra that really absorbed Napoléon's attention. He wanted it to be the most splendid street in all of Europe, and, characteristically, he wanted it to be called the Rue Napoléon. The returning Bourbon monarchs saw things differently, and Napoléon's pride and joy became the Rue de la Paix.

Ironically, the Place Vendôme itself was built by Louis XIV, and originally it was his statue, not Napoléon's, that presided here. But, no longer. At the center of this fabled plaza, which some feel is akin to the center of the universe, now stands Napoléon Bonaparte himself, on his famed column (which grandly celebrates his victory at Austerlitz). He is dressed in a toga, like Caesar, and seems to be enjoying himself.

And why not? He succeeded magnificently in his tussle with history, stamping his name and achievements on collective memory much like the Greek and Roman heroes he so adored. In the process, he dared to make Paris—the legendary city of legendary monarchs—his own.

NOTE: The museum in which you can find the imperial bees is the Musée de Notre-Dame de Paris, 10 Rue du Cloître-Notre-Dame, 4th.

VIII

STARS

The Divine Miss B

FIRST AND FOREMOST SARAH BERNHARDT WAS A STAR. An international superstar, whose overwhelming drive, ambition, and genius for publicity kept her aloft for a spectacular fifty years—a run that today's superstars might envy.

Of course she was both beautiful and talented—sublimely so. For years, she was rightly recognized as the preeminent tragic actress of her day. But as she so shrewdly recognized, beauty and talent alone were not enough to send her to the stratosphere, or to keep her there in defiance of younger rivals, fickle audiences, and changing times. With clear-eyed realism, she recognized that audiences would not turn out in droves in Chicago and Istanbul to see an actress, no matter how famous, perform in a language they did not understand unless there was something more to draw them. This special allure was the legend she created, the aura and the excitement with which she surrounded herself and which her audiences shared for the magical moments they were in her presence.

The legend was an extraordinary one, spiced with melo-drama, extravagant luxury, and a scandalous number of lovers. Although she smoothed over the rougher edges of her biography for her adoring public, Bernhardt had been schooled for scandal from the start. Born in 1844 on the Left Bank of Paris (probably in the attractive residence at 5 Rue de l'Ecole-de-Médecine, 6th), she was the eldest daughter of a pretty Dutch courtesan who had clawed her way out of poverty and into the arms of a series of wealthy protectors, one of whom (we do not know which) was Sarah's father.

Expected to earn a living, Sarah first turned to acting—a likely enough profession at a time when actresses were expected to have dubious morals, and the casting couch was an assumed part of the job. Fresh out of the Conservatoire, she made her debut at the Comédie-Française—starting at the top. But she was young and inexperienced, and did herself no favors with her volcanic temper, more suitable to a diva. Discouraged by cold treatment and bad reviews, she left the theater for a series of adventures, one of which left her pregnant with her beloved son, Maurice.

Unquestionably, Sarah could have been wildly successful at her mother's profession, but, fortunately, she decided to give the theater another try. The director of the Théâtre de l'Odéon gave her a chance, and she persuaded him to keep her on until, after two long years, she at last had a hit. This lovely Left Bank theater, located in Place de l'Odéon (6th), adjacent to the Luxembourg Gardens, is where Sarah Bernhardt first became a success.

The Franco-Prussian War and the subsequent upheavals of the Paris Commune interrupted her career, but as soon as Paris got itself back together, she returned to the stage—this time in a memorable revival of Victor Hugo's *Ruy Blas*. Soon after, she returned in triumph to the Comédie-Française.

Not only did she bring a fresh perspective on acting to this staid old institution, refusing to perform in the old-fashioned declamatory manner, but she began to introduce Paris—and the world—to a legend-in-the-making, much of which was created especially for public consumption. It was now that she revealed that she studied her roles while reclining in a satin-lined coffin, and she even had herself photographed sleeping there. She had herself photographed in a wide variety of other activities as well, including sculpting, for which she dramatically posed in white silk pants. Theatergoing Parisians were already accustomed to seeing Sarah Bernhardt's legs—she had, after all, achieved her first major success at the Théâtre de l'Odéon in a trouser role. Still, the nineteenth century was generally unaccustomed to such exposure, and such photos sold widely, adding to her notoriety.

Legends require furs and jewels, with which Bernhardt regally swathed herself. Legends also require suitably sumptuous surroundings, and soon after her triumphant return to the Comédie-Française, she built herself an opulent palace, at 35/37 Rue Fortuny (17th), in the fashionable area just north of Parc Monceau. Here she decorated with abandon, inviting her artist friends and hangers-on to indulge their ornate fancies.

As her fame grew, her position at the Comédie-Française seemed increasingly restrictive. At last breaking out on her own, she bought the Théâtre de la Porte Saint-Martin (16 Boulevard Saint-Martin, 10th) and formed her own company. Henceforth she would be her own manager and leading lady.

The history of this particular theater, located adjacent to the Porte Saint-Martin, must have appealed to her. After all, Victor Hugo had

Painting of Sarah Bernhardt by Georges Jules Victor Clairin

enjoyed some of his greatest successes here. Still, it was a huge house to fill. After a series of box-office setbacks, which forced her to sell her beloved home on Rue Fortuny and move to cheaper quarters, Bernhardt sold this theater and moved virtually next door to the smaller yet quite elegant Théâtre de la Renaissance (20 Boulevard Saint-Martin, 10th). She also launched a theater tour of America—a venture that proved to be a gold mine, drawing her back to the New World again and again.

Preceded by sizzling stories of her flamboyant lifestyle, Bernhardt hit New York like a storm. Her elegance and beauty

Théâtre de la Renaissance

seduced, while the luxury to which she was accustomed left Americans gasping. Once front and center in the public's attention, she made sure that this translated into success at the box office. Anticipating that Americans would understand little of what was being said on stage, which remained entirely in French, she made sure to entertain her audience visually, providing her productions with spectacular costumes (her gown for *La Dame aux Camélias* was embroidered in pearls). Treated to spectacle both on stage and off, Americans swooned with delight.

Traveling was difficult, even with a luxuriously appointed private train to provide accommodations in the remoter corners of the country. But Bernhardt gamely pressed on, playing in dozens of cities and towns before returning to France. She made a fortune in the process, and was able to buy herself another Paris house, at 56 Boulevard Pereire (17th).

She also sold the Théâtre de la Renaissance (it was too small) and bought the Théâtre des Nations on the Place du Châtelet (4th), renaming it the Théâtre Sarah Bernhardt (it is now the Théâtre de la Ville). It was the only theater in which she performed during the remaining years of her life.

She lived long and fully, performing to the end despite a leg amputation, and filling her house on Boulevard Pereire with mementoes of her travels, including a menagerie of animals. By the time of her death, in 1923, she had become outdated, yet remained a legend. Her funeral cortege to Père-Lachaise cemetery passed through streets lined with thousands of mourners, who showered her coffin with affection and flowers. It was a fitting final performance, and one she would have adored.

NOTE: Sarah Bernhardt is buried in Père-Lachaise cemetery (20th), along with a host of other celebrities, including Abélard and Héloïse, Frédéric Chopin, Gertrude Stein, Molière, Oscar Wilde, Marcel Proust, Honoré de Balzac, Isadora Duncan, Amedeo Modigliani, Edith Piaf, Yves Montand, Colette, and of course, Jim Morrison. You will find Bernhardt along the far edge of section 44, in the midst of this vast city of the dead, where she undoubtedly reigns as queen.

21.

IT IS TUCKED AWAY, DOWN A PASSAGE AND BEYOND THE
bedrooms of Marcel Proust and Anna de Noailles. Turn left at
the ballroom, and there, at the end of a corridor, you will find
yourself facing one of the most astonishing little shops in Paris.

You have navigated the farthest reaches of the Musée Carnavalet (23 Rue de Sévigné, 3rd) and are now gazing at the *fin de
siècle* jewelry store of Georges Fouquet, an Art Nouveau confec-
tion straight from a *Belle Epoque* land of dreams. Now a permanent resident of the Carnavalet, this exotic boutique once
resided on Rue Royale, where Parisians of wealth and style
flocked to ogle and acquire the latest in expensive baubles.

Fouquet's jewel box—a carefully crafted concoction of pea-
cocks, flowers, and lightly clad beauties—was the creation of
Alphonse Mucha, Paris' famed poster artist, who almost
overnight propelled his highly romantic fantasies to the front
ranks of fashion. By 1901, when he designed Fouquet's *bijouterie*,

Mucha's curved, flowing lines and long-tressed ladies had become so famous that many Parisians referred to Art Nouveau itself simply as the "Mucha style."

This style seems to have been a sudden inspiration, the gift of a moment, for there is no trace of it in Mucha's earlier work. Perhaps his upbringing imposed a certain conservatism, for this Czech artist was born into modest circumstances, in a family where choosing an artistic career was of itself revolutionary. Setting his hand to everything from stage sets to tombstones, young Mucha worked tirelessly but without flair. When at last he found a patron willing to sponsor his art studies—first in Munich, then in Paris—the young artist did little to distinguish himself.

After a while the wealthy patron cut off support, leaving Mucha virtually penniless in Paris. Fortunately, a friend took pity and found him a room at 13 Rue de la Grande-Chaumière (6th), above Madame Charlotte's Crémerie. This marked a crucial turning point, for Madame Charlotte and her Crémerie (which has long since disappeared) played much the same role in succoring Paris' starving artists in the 1880s and '90s as did La Ruche and Le Bateau-Lavoir a decade or so later. Madame Charlotte—a buxom widow with a small pension and a heart of gold—made it her business to feed and care for her extended family, which regularly assembled for the food, camaraderie, and maternal concern she generously provided.

Among the odd assortment that showed up at the Crémerie during Mucha's tenure were the much-misunderstood artist, Paul Gauguin, and the touchy Swedish playwright, August

Strindberg. Gauguin made off for Tahiti, while Strindberg took long walks with Mucha through Montparnasse cemetery, during which they chatted about their common interest in the occult. When Gauguin returned, broke, Mucha generously offered to share his studio with him. Gauguin accepted, and this astonishingly disparate duo worked together for a time—each in his own corner.

By now Mucha had achieved a certain amount of recognition as an illustrator, and his fortunes were improving. Befitting his bigger income, he moved to larger quarters across the street at No. 8 (a plaque notes that Gauguin once had a studio at this address, but neglects to mention Mucha). There he purchased a harmonium, which on at least one occasion Gauguin—clad only in briefs and shirt—tried to play (Mucha captured this bizarre moment on film).

Life generally was looking better, but Christmas of 1894 began on a bleak note. Alone once more and without work, Mucha found himself proofing some lithographs for a vacationing friend. He was just finishing up when the manager of the print shop rushed in. Sarah Bernhardt—the divine Sarah herself—had just telephoned to demand a new poster for her current play, *Gismonda,* by New Year's Day.

It was impossible! There were no available artists who could do such a job. And then the manager looked thoughtfully at Mucha. Could this young man, still virtually an unknown, produce a work that would please the great Bernhardt? It was worth a try.

Mucha was more than willing, and set off for the glorious

Théâtre de la Renaissance, where *Gismonda* was playing. (Still very much in business, at 20 Boulevard Saint-Martin, 10th, this fine old theater sports a flamboyant array of nudes that have bedecked it since 1872.) Enchanted with Sarah, Mucha immediately set to work creating the poster that would change his life.

Where did the ideas come from that set him off in this completely new direction, so unlike anything he had ever done before? No one knows, although it is true that for some time Mucha had been soaking up ideas from his colleagues at the Crémerie. These influences would have included the new Symbolism and the Japanese art that were sweeping avant-garde Paris, as well as the curved, organic elements of Art Nouveau. Even Strindberg's mysticism and some of the techniques that Gauguin employed may have seeped into his subconscious.

But Mucha's *Gismonda* poster was something uniquely and even startlingly his own. The manager and owner of the print shop were in fact horrified by what they saw, and sent the poster off to Sarah only because they felt they had no other choice. Sunk in gloom, Mucha awaited the verdict.

Sarah loved it. Summoning Mucha to the theater, she immediately signed him to a six-year contract to design not only posters but also sets and costumes. When Mucha's *Gismonda* poster appeared on New Year's Day, it became the talk of the town. Nothing like it had ever been seen before, and the public scrambled to get copies. (A shrewd businesswoman, Sarah ordered 4,000 more to sell at profit.)

Mucha continued to work with Sarah when she went on to open her Théâtre Sarah Bernhardt, at what now is the

Théâtre de la Ville in the Place du Châtelet. He also became a successful designer, painter, and sculptor. But it is as a poster artist that he is best remembered, and where he achieved his greatest fame. Here he established his trademark celebration of beautiful women—ravishing beauties, with swirling gowns and long, flowing hair.

Mucha eventually left the Rue de la Grande-Chaumière for larger and more elegant quarters at nearby 6 Rue du Val-de-Grâce, 5th (a commemorative plaque marks this still-lovely address, in the shadow of the magnificent church of Val-de-Grâce). He married a beautiful Czech art student, traveled to America, and then left Paris for good, returning to the land of his birth. Here he spent the last thirty years of his life, painting the epic history of his homeland.

By the end, all the posters and pursuits of his Paris years had become for him a frivolity. Yet in retrospect, these years were far more important than he realized. For the swirling flowers and flowing tresses of Mucha's maidens created a special world, whose magic still exerts its considerable charm today.

Stained-glass medallion by Alphonse Mucha at bijouterie Georges Fouquet, Musée Carnavalet

22.

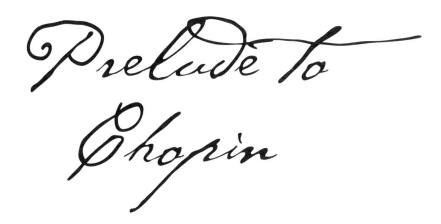

OH, TO BE YOUNG AND TO BE IN PARIS! LIKE COUNTLESS others, Fryderyk Chopin had the same dream, departing for Paris in 1830, when he was twenty years old.

He was half-French and half-Polish, his father being a Frenchman whose fortunes had taken him in exactly the reverse geographical direction. The son dearly loved his Polish homeland, but by 1830 political events had made life there intolerable. Fryderyk (Frédéric, in French) Chopin would spend most of the rest of his life in Paris.

He never forgot the land of his birth, but it was difficult not to fall in love with Paris. The thrill in his tone as he described his first modest apartment, at 27 Boulevard Poissonnière (2nd), is unmistakable: "You wouldn't believe what a charming place I have," he wrote a friend, with all the enthusiasm of a college student. "A little room, handsomely furnished in mahogany, with a little balcony on the boulevard from which I can see from Montmartre to the Panthéon and all along the finest districts."

People envied him his view but not his stairs, he confessed of this fifth-floor walk-up, whose wrought-iron balcony is still clearly visible from the street below. Although the building has been turned into office space and a store, it's worth a visit just to see Chopin's immediate neighborhood. Centered around the bustling and fashionable Boulevard Montmartre and Boulevard des Italiens, it is still is a fascinating place. On Boulevard Montmartre, for example, you will find mazes of glass-roofed passageways lined with expensive period-inspired restaurants and boutiques. The nineteenth-century equivalent of deluxe indoor shopping malls, these galleries have for almost two centuries drawn wealthy Parisians, to shop, sip coffee, or merely promenade the elegant covered walkways. Well-established before Chopin even reached Paris, the extensive Passage des Panoramas (to the south) and Passage Jouffroy (to the north, continuing into Passage Verdeau) provided much to interest and amuse this young dandy, who dressed in the latest fashion and soon acclimated himself to Paris society, moving in its highest circles.

Within just a few months after arriving in Paris, Chopin had established himself sufficiently as a chamber pianist for the elite—and piano teacher to their children—that he was able to move to better quarters at 4 Cité Bergère (9th), just around the corner from his former lodgings. Located in a quiet passage just off Rue du Faubourg-Montmartre, his first-floor apartment (all traces of which have vanished) gave him more of the peace he required to compose. It also offered ground-floor convenience for this notoriously delicate young man and his wealthy students.

A year later, he was doing well enough that he could move again, this time to 5 Rue de la Chaussée-d'Antin (9th), in the heart of the neighborhood known as New Athens (acclaimed for its many successful artists, musicians, and writers). Furnishing it expensively, according to his exacting tastes, Chopin lived there until 1836, when he moved to even better quarters farther up the street, at No. 38. (Neither of these dwellings still exists.)

It was while he lived at No. 38 that Chopin met and began his famous relationship with novelist George Sand. Following their return from a disastrous winter in Majorca (where Chopin almost died from the rain and cold, but managed to finish his Preludes), he moved to 5 Rue Tronchet (8th), just behind the church of the Madeleine. At the same time, Sand and her two children moved into two small houses at the back of a garden courtyard at 16 Rue

Drawing of Frederic Chopin by George Sand

By permission of the Music Division,
The New York Public Library for the Performing Arts,
Astor, Lenox and Tilden Foundations

Jean-Baptiste Pigalle (9th), where Chopin eventually joined her. No trace of the garden courtyard or the two residences that Sand and Chopin occupied remains behind the doors of No. 16. But nearby, the lovely recessed garden home of artist Ary Scheffer (now the Musée de la Vie Romantique, 16 Rue Chaptal, 9th), where Sand and Chopin were frequent visitors, gives a feeling for what their quarters on Rue Jean-Baptiste Pigalle may have looked like.

Wearying of their cramped lodgings, in 1842 Chopin and Sand moved to more comfortable quarters in nearby Square d'Orléans (Rue Taitbout at Rue Saint-Lazare, 9th)—an elegant enclave surrounding a series of linked courtyards. Beautifully preserved, this site is well worth a visit even without its claim to fame. Here, Chopin lived at No. 9, while Sand lived at No. 5. Madame Sand moved out in 1847, after the couple's traumatic breakup, but Chopin stayed on for two more years, almost until his death.

The very address of Chopin's last dwelling, a lavish apartment at 12 Place Vendôme (1st), gives a feeling for the kind of luxury to which he had become accustomed. Unquestionably a success, he nevertheless had always outspent his income, derived largely from teaching. By the end of his life, when he became too ill to teach, he would have died destitute had it not been for the financial support of his devoted Scottish pupil, Jane Stirling. Here, in a spacious first-floor apartment overlooking a large inner courtyard, he died on October 17, 1849. He was only thirty-nine years old.

Nearly three thousand people attended his funeral at the

church of the Madeleine, delayed until October 30 in order to organize a performance of Mozart's Requiem, as Chopin himself had wished. Afterwards, he was buried in the fashionable cemetery of Père-Lachaise. A sculpture of a grieving Calliope marks his tomb—one of the most visited sites in the cemetery.

Less well-known is his room at the Polish museum, the Musée Adam-Mickiewicz (6 Quai d'Orléans, on the Ile Saint-Louis). Although open only during limited hours and shadowed with nineteenth-century gloom, its Salle Chopin has some fascinating items.

"You find here [in Paris]," Chopin wrote, shortly after his arrival, "the greatest splendor, the greatest filthiness, the greatest virtue and the greatest vice." And yet, overall, Paris delighted him. "I have the finest musicians and opera in the world," he added, "and shall perhaps stay here longer than I intended—not because things have been too easy for me but because they *may* gradually turn out well."

A bittersweet observation, given the mix of extraordinary achievement, lasting fame, and early death that was about to come.

23.

THERE IS A PLACE DEEP IN THE HEART OF THE 13TH arrondissement where a small wood follows the course of the now-underground river Bièvre. Here long ago, during a violent thunderstorm, a tormented young man stabbed to death a beautiful shepherdess who had spurned him.

If this sounds like something straight out of Victor Hugo, then you are not far wrong. For the wood is part of the beautiful Square René-le-Gall, which spreads over the former Champ de l'Alouette, or Field of the Lark, where the young shepherdess died. Attracted by the story's dark drama, Hugo used this spot as the site that so magnetically drew Marius, the yearning young lover of *Les Misérables.*

Hugo set his powerful novels in real and frequently edgy settings, but it was not only the drama of these sites that appealed to him. Sometimes, as in the case of the Lark's Field, he was paying tribute to personal attachments as well. Here, along quiet and shady Rue de Croulebarbe, he passed many pleasant hours with friends at a tavern owned by a certain Madame Grégoire. This quaint old building, still well preserved at No. 41, has for many years housed a Basque restaurant, the Auberge Etchegorry, where an old-fashioned coziness—and memories of Hugo—linger on.

There are many such memories, even more than two centuries after Hugo's birth. Poet, playwright, novelist, artist, politician, and statesman, this titanic Frenchman left a massive legacy of words and deeds, including the huge literary embrace he cast around Paris, his beloved home.

Born in Besançon, near the Swiss border, Hugo—the youngest son of an officer in Bonaparte's army—arrived in the City of Light at the age of two. His mother, a confirmed royalist, had given up on her marriage, leaving Major Hugo to his mistress and his wars. Settling in Paris with her three sons, Madame Hugo soon acquired a lover of her own, who plotted against Napoléon and ended up facing a firing squad. In the midst of this festering family life, little Victor found refuge in the luxuriously overgrown garden behind his home on the Impasse des Feuillantines, 5th (Rue des Feuillantines still exists, but not the Impasse or the house). Here, in the shadow of Val-de-Grâce and the Panthéon, he reveled in Nature and grew to adolescence.

But the garden was only a temporary refuge. Back and forth young Victor went, between mother and father (now a general), between royalist and Napoleonic sympathies, between Paris, Italy, and Spain. Even Paris at first offered little stability, as one home followed another in depressing secession, leaving the lovely garden of the Feuillantines well behind.

In the midst of all this turmoil, young Hugo began to write and found that he was good at it—winning a major prize from the Académie Française when he was only fifteen. Along with his older brothers (who shared his literary ambitions, if not his talent), he founded a literary review, which he filled with an avalanche of poetry and prose. Yet even these triumphs could not entirely distract from his family's ongoing troubles, including the dismal evidence that his brother Eugène was going mad. Indeed, on the day of Victor's wedding to Adèle Foucher, Eugène permanently slipped over the boundary into insanity and spent the rest of his brief life in a padded cell.

Life for young Victor Hugo was beginning to look a lot like a Victor Hugo novel. Still, there were sunny moments, and by his mid-twenties, Hugo had achieved an enviable literary reputation and the income to go with it. Moving with his wife and daughter to a lovely apartment and garden on Rue Notre-Dame-des-Champs, 6th (now obliterated by the current Métro stop), he began to embrace a more liberal politics. He also began to write plays, making his triumphal debut at the Comédie-Française with *Hernani,* where he achieved a complete coup for the daring new Romantic over traditional Classical style. A bas-relief of Hugo, along with three other French immortals (Racine, Corneille, and Molière), currently decorates the front of the Comédie-Française on Place André-Malraux (2 Rue de Richelieu, 1st).

With a growing family, Victor and Adèle moved to larger

quarters at Rue Jean-Goujon (8th), a prime Right Bank location near the Seine. Here, Hugo continued his dramatic triumphs at both the Comédie-Française and the Théâtre de la Porte Saint-Martin (a fine old theater at 16 Boulevard Saint-Martin, 10th, rebuilt in all its glory after the Commune put the torch to the original in 1871).

It was the 1831 publication of Hugo's astonishing novel, *Notre-Dame de Paris*, that really sent up the fireworks, announcing the arrival of a major literary star. Huge, rambling, and fairly dripping with emotion, this dark Romantic tale quickly became a blockbuster, translated into countless foreign languages, including English, where it was retitled *The Hunchback of Notre-Dame.*

Hugo hated the English title. The focus of his novel had never been Quasimodo, the monstrous hunchback, but Notre-Dame itself and the slum-filled Paris that surrounded it. Passionately drawn to the medieval architecture and poverty-mired denizens of this ancient quarter, Hugo turned his novel into a not-so-subtle demand for social justice as well as an ode to the past. After centuries of decay, Notre-Dame now vaulted to the forefront of public attention. Saving this neglected twelfth-century masterpiece suddenly became the most popular of causes, and Hugo did not hesitate to ride the wave he had created, prodding restoration efforts that eventually preserved the cathedral.

Soon after publication of *Notre-Dame de Paris*, Hugo moved his family to 6 Place des Vosges (4th), now the Maison de Victor Hugo and the most well-known of his many Paris residences. Here, in this extraordinary seventeenth-century square—which he shrugged off as architecturally uninteresting—Hugo lived from 1832 to 1848 in the height of Gothic comfort. During this time he struck up a liaison with actress Juliette Drouet that would last the rest of his life, while wife Adèle found refuge with Hugo's friend, the writer and critic Charles Augustin Sainte-Beuve. This could not have been the happiest of households, but Hugo continued to pour out torrents of words, including an initial sketch of *Les Misérables*. He did not complete it until his long years of exile on the Isles of Jersey and Guernsey (1851–70), where he sought refuge from the increasingly repressive government of Napoléon III.

Writing far from Paris, Hugo recreated in minute detail the Paris he had known, and which even then was disappearing. When he returned to Paris in triumph in 1870, he found a city he no longer recognized, set out along broad boulevards that served a decidedly military as well as aesthetic purpose. Hugo's Paris, the old Paris of medieval alleys and sordid slums, had gone for good.

And yet it is still possible to find pockets of the Paris of which Hugo wrote—albeit in considerably cleaner clothes. In addition to the Field of the Lark, one of the most interesting is the site of the Corinth (1st), the tavern in *Les Misérables* where Hugo's students threw up their ill-fated barricade. Hugo gives precise directions, but these are based on what used to be—before Haussmann and the remodeled Les Halles. Yet you can still find traces of the narrow alleyways that once wound through here, from the spaghetti-like route of Rue Mondétour to the tiny Rues de la Petite-Truanderie and Grande-Truanderie, which meet in an equally diminutive square. The Corinth probably stood at the corner of Rue Rambuteau and Rue Mondétour, in the now-gentrified area just to the north of Les Halles.

Much like the dramatic and emotion-fraught books he wrote, Hugo's later years reflected a particularly Gothic stew of heights and depths, tragedy and triumph. While piling up mountains of honors, including election to the Senate, membership in the Académie Française, and worldwide literary and political acclaim, he suffered the death of his beloved elder daughter and the insanity of his youngest. And although praised to Olympian heights for his godlike character and contributions to society, Hugo constantly courted scandal with his epic womanizing.

Yet his public continued to adore him. His last address, at what now is 124 Avenue Victor Hugo (16th), marks the site

124 Avenue Victor Hugo

where crowds of more than a half million people paraded past, for hours, to celebrate his eightieth birthday (a striking bas-relief of an elderly Hugo glares down from over the door). And when he died here in 1885 (his deathbed is now in the Maison de Victor-Hugo), Paris gave him a blowout funeral, including burial in the Panthéon—an extraordinary honor, even though he had once condemned the place as a "wretched copy of Saint Peter's in Rome."

But no one minded—especially not the Parisians. For he was *their* Victor Hugo. And his Paris—the Paris of Esmeralda and Jean Valjean—would live forever.

IX

FIRST IMPRESSIONS

Cradle of Impressionism

"I HAVE A DREAM," CLAUDE MONET WROTE IN 1869, envisioning the magic glow of light on water that enveloped the Grenouillère, the famed floating café on the banks of the Seine, near Paris. So far, he added, he had not progressed beyond some "bad sketches." Yet he still held fast to his dream.

Pierre-Auguste Renoir, who had been staying nearby, also shared the dream, and at length the two young artists agreed to paint the scene together. Here, working side by side, they ushered in a completely new way of observing—and painting. Using quick strokes of juxtaposed colors, they captured the fleeting effect of light on water and the joyous effervescence of the moment. The Impressionist Movement had begun.

Rejecting the formalism of the reigning school of academic painting, which delighted in careful renditions of historic tableaux recreated in the studio, these revolutionary painters wanted more than anything to capture real life, painted in haste and out-of-doors. "One should be able to draw a man falling from the fifth floor, before he hits the ground," one enthusiast is said to have exclaimed. Without taking him literally, the new Impressionists nevertheless understood the necessity for a total change in subject matter as well as method, selecting subjects from the constant flow of everyday life rather than those that needed to be carefully arranged.

In practice, this meant a new focus on the mundane, from country roads to domestic pleasures. It also meant a new attention to ordinary people as they went about their everyday lives. At the Grenouillère, Renoir and Monet captured on canvas not only the effect of light on water, but also the palpable pleasure of Parisians holidaying on the Seine.

Renoir again caught this relaxed and festive mood at two other nearby locations: the working-class dancers of his *Dance at Bougival*, and the casual conviviality of his *Luncheon of the Boating Party*—a moment of sun-drenched bliss on the balcony of the famed Maison Fournaise, in Chatou.

Like the Grenouillère, the Maison Fournaise—which Renoir called "the most beautiful spot in all the environs of Paris"—owed its existence to the railroad, which since the 1830s had provided easy access to this delightful area just west of Paris, from Chatou to Bougival and beyond. Boating on the Seine, as well as strolling along its banks, soon become a major leisure activity for Parisians of all classes, who democratically mixed and mingled there. Sensing good business possibilities, a barge-man and boatbuilder by the name of Alphonse Fournaise built an open-air café and small hotel on the Ile de Chatou. With the help of his daughter, Alphonsine, and his son, Alphonse, he also developed a boat rental business. Soon his enterprise, the Maison Fournaise, became a meeting place for writers, artists, and celebrities of all sorts, including Guy de Maupassant, who immortalized it in several of his short stories.

When twentieth-century bicycling sent boating into oblivion as a Sunday-afternoon pastime, the Maison Fournaise, as well as the Grenouillère and a string of other *guinguettes*, or river cafés and dance halls, went into decline. Decades passed, and the town of Chatou at length bought and (with the assistance of public and private funds, including Les Amis de la Maison Fournaise and the USA-based Friends of French Art) restored the fading Fournaise building, which has recently reopened as a restaurant and museum. Located just below the Pont de Chatou, the Maison Fournaise is once again a popular destination for a leisurely lunch or the start of a stroll along paths that the Impressionists themselves once took.

Whether or not you decide to lunch on the same balcony immortalized by Renoir, you will want to visit the Fournaise Museum, a small but fascinating introduction to the spirit of the Impressionist era. Here you will find rotating exhibitions of historic photos, paintings of Chatou (by lesser-known artists), portraits of Alphonse Fournaise and friends, plus displays that recreate the Maison's glory days, such as its original murals and tableware. You will even find one of the surprisingly shallow and tippy-looking boats. Be sure to pick up a map of "Le Chemin des Impressionnistes" on your way out the door.

The Ile de Chatou merges into the Ile de Bougival, whose

northern end has been most appropriately named the Ile des Impressionnistes. Save this island route for your return trip and instead follow the shoreline walk to the sign (complete with reproduced Renoir painting) marking the site of the now-vanished Grenouillère, which originally straddled the wasp-waist of the island here. Augmented by floating pontoons, the Grenouillère's café, dance floor, and swimming facilities attracted crowds of pleasure-seeking Parisians well before Monet and Renoir decided to set up their easels on the site. In fact, Gustave Courbet had already painted here, and Edouard Manet used its grounds as his inspiration for *Déjeuner sur l'herbe* (which, given its infamous nude picnicker, was most under-standably painted in his studio).

Guy de Maupassant, who was just as dearly attached to the Grenouillère as to the Maison Fournaise, rapturously described the giant trees shading the spot, calling it "the most delicious park in the world." Most beloved, perhaps, of all its charms was the Grenouillère's tiny islet—sometimes referred to as the "pot of flowers," but more commonly known as the "Camembert" because of its resemblance to a small and delectable round of Norman cheese. This circlet of greenery—the focus of Renoir's and Monet's famous paintings—disappeared along with the rest of the Grenouillère under backfill in the 1920s.

Most fortunately the setting's beauty has remained, and plans are underway to recreate the famous watering place (you can even glimpse the rebuilt "Camembert" island—now land-locked—on your return route). But for now, you can indulge in more concrete mementos at the nearby Grenouillère Museum.

Here, on the ground floor of Maison Joséphine (the historic house where the widowed Joséphine lived with her two children before marrying Napoléon Bonaparte), Les Amis de la Grenouillère (Friends of the Grenouillère) have created a choice collection of cartoons, photos, paintings, costumes, and even a café setting for Impressionist buffs. Complete with a small reproduction of the Grenouillère itself, the museum provides a far racier view of goings-on at the "Camembert" than either Monet or Renoir let on.

After returning to the river, continue this dreamy amble to the Pont de Bougival. Here, from an exit at the bridge's middle, you can return via the Ile de Bougival and the Grenouillère site, keeping an eye out for the rebuilt "Camembert." Or you can cross the bridge into the attractive hillside town of Bougival, which served as a beauty-filled retreat for a number of Impressionist painters.

Bougival once had its own riverside dance halls and festivities, which Renoir so memorably painted. In addition, if you continue a short distance westward down the Bougival side of the Seine, you will reach a small bridge leading to the Bougival locks (*écluses*), a favorite subject of several of the Impressionists, including Alfred Sisley. Sisley used this part of the Seine to study the effect of light on sky and water, but he also enjoyed the river traffic, which is just as much fun to watch today.

As you let your gaze rise from the river to the steep hills above Bougival, keep in mind that soon after Monet and Renoir triggered the Impressionist revolution at the Grenouillère, Camille Pissarro made his own artistic breakthrough as he

painted with Monet in these very hills. In the years that followed, Pissarro, together with Sisley, painted in the quiet lanes
and byways of this section of the Seine, from Port-Marly to
Marly-le-Roi and Louveciennes, experimenting with the effect
of light on cottages and trees, clouds and snow. And while
Renoir may have made his name painting people and portraits,
he was also drawn to these quiet landscapes and country roads.

Since the heart of this picturesque area stretches along
heights that rise well above the Seine, the easiest approach is
from inland, either from Marly-le-Roi or Louveciennes.
Although both are now prosperous suburbs of Paris, they have
managed to retain the serenity and particular quality of light as
well as many of the exact sites that attracted the Impressionists
here more than a century ago.

To follow the Impressionists' path from either of these
towns, start at the railway station. Either will do, although
you may prefer to start your wander in Louveciennes, which
has more of a beginning feel to it. Just outside the Louveciennes station, a sign complete with a Pissarro reproduction
alerts you that he painted this exact view in 1870—only
months after Monet and Renoir introduced Impressionism's
possibilities at the Grenouillère.

From here, where you can see an aqueduct in the distance,
you are within a breath of the little village of Voisins, now part
of Louveciennes. The early Impressionists found Voisins
charming, and Monet and Renoir as well as Sisley and Pissarro
couldn't resist the effect of light on its country cottages,
whether in summer sun or winter snow.

If you follow the village's narrow, winding main street (Rue de Voisins), you will cross the Rue de la Machine, part of the route along which Louis XIV's awe-inspiring Machine de Marly pumped water from the Seine to the grand royal *châteaux* at Marly and Versailles. Both Pissarro and Sisley frequented this route, as two more Impressionist site markers attest. Further up the Rue de Voisins you will find another Pissarro site, and at the top of the hill, where it dead ends at the Route de Versailles, you will find the place where Renoir painted the alley of trees that still lines each side of this old road.

Along the nearby Avenue Saint-Martin you will find the sites where Pissarro painted his *Entrance to the Village of Voisins*, and Sisley painted the Aqueduct of Marly. Nowadays, trees half hide the aqueduct, but take a few more steps down the road and you will see the huge structure rising impressively above you. Follow this seventeenth-century landmark to its end, and you will be at the Parc de Marly. Here you can wander the park's full length, enjoying the alleys of trees and remaining ponds while envisioning the grandeur of yesteryear. The Impressionists loved these grounds (look for another Pissarro site beneath the trees) as well as the adjoining town of Marly-le-Roi. At the park's tip there remains an old watering place, or *abreuvoir*, which Sisley painted again and again during the two years he lived here, paying particular attention, as always, to the ever-changing clouds and sky.

In Marly-le-Roi you will find a Tourist Office, train station, and yet another Sisley site, near the Hôtel de Ville, where the artist painted the effects of light on snow—a moment of deep quiet and tranquility. This can be either the end or the beginning of your wander in this portion of the Cradle of Impressionism—a peaceful and sheltered landscape above the Seine, where a revolutionary group of painters found both truth and beauty in the magic of each fleeting moment.

NOTE: To reach Maison Fournaise (Ile de Chatou), take RER line A1 to Rueil-Malmaison. From the station walk toward the Chatou bridge, following the exit ramp at the middle of the bridge to the island. To start your Impressionist walk, return to the bridge and continue toward Chatou, looping back under the bridge to follow the riverside path westward toward Croissy-sur-Seine. At the Grenouillère marker, turn right up the steps through the park, then right again to the Musée Grenouillère (ground floor of Maison Joséphine, 6 bis Grande Rue, Croissy-sur-Seine). Returning to the Seine, continue to the Bougival bridge. Halfway across you will find an exit ramp that descends to the Ile de Bougival, where you will find two plaques marking sites where Monet and Berthe Morisot painted. Follow the island path along the northern branch of the Seine to the still-lovely Grenouillère site. From here follow the path to the Parc Natural, returning via the Chatou bridge to the Rueil-Malmaison station.

If instead of returning directly from the Bougival bridge you decide to view the Bougival locks, descend at the Bougival side of the river and continue west for several blocks toward Port-Marly and the Ile de la Loge. En route you will encounter a site marker for the Fauvist painter, Maurice de Vlaminck, as well as two Sisley site markers at the foot of the small bridge leading to the Ile de la Loge. Here, follow the road to the right to find all three locks (still active) and another Sisley site marker. Total circuit distance to and from the Rueil-Malmaison station, including the Bougival locks, is about five miles.

To reach Louveciennes or Marly-le-Roi, take the SNCF from Gare Saint-Lazare. The Marly-le-Roi Tourist Office is located just outside the park entrance, at 2 Avenue des Combattants.

25.
The Forgotten Impressionist

THE NEXT TIME YOU ARE NEAR THE PONT-NEUF AND feel like exploring, turn down the Right Bank along the Quai de la Mégisserie to No. 14. There, flanked by carved caryatids, stands one of the many huge carriage doors that still dot this section of Paris. Press the buzzer and enter. Here in the shadows you will find four bas-relief medallions of a young woman, done in classic style.

The medallions' sculptor, Aimé Millet, was famous, and the woman quite obviously was a beauty. But who was she?

Millet's model was Berthe Morisot, one of six founders of the Impressionist movement (along with Claude Monet, Edgar Degas, Pierre-Auguste Renoir, Camille Pissarro, and Alfred Sisley). Despite fame and even notoriety during the height of her career, she largely disappeared from public memory following her death, slipping into shadows that were perhaps as much of her own making as that of the intensely traditional society in which she lived.

Born in 1841 into a family of high-level civil servants, Morisot was raised in upper-middle-class comfort in Passy, then on the western outskirts of Paris. You can still explore the streets of her childhood homes (Rue Scheffer at Rue Vineuse, 16 Rue Benjamin-Franklin, and 7 Rue Guichard—all within several blocks of each other in the 16th arrondissement) to grasp the privileged milieu in which she lived her entire life.

When she and her sister showed a distinct flair for art, the Morisot parents unhesitatingly provided both daughters with accomplished teachers, including the well-known sculptor, Millet. After all, it was considered appropriate for a young woman in the Morisots' circle to paint or play a musical instrument competently.

But while Monsieur and Madame Morisot were intent on burnishing their daughters' social graces, Berthe soon realized that she possessed an ability and need for expression that far outstripped the conventional amateurism that her social standing and gender permitted. Even more dismaying, she was developing an entirely unconventional way of painting. Having rejected the static stage-sets of the studio for the more revolutionary out-of-doors, she was already striving to capture the fleeting moments of everyday life—the style that derisive critics would soon call Impressionism. Monet, Renoir, and Pissarro, painting in tandem, were simultaneously pressing for this same goal. But unable to spend time with her fellow artists at local cafés, Berthe Morisot developed her Impressionist vision and techniques on her own.

Driven by an increasingly clear—and radical—vision of what to paint and how, Berthe was plagued with constraints. Although the Salon opened its prestigious doors to her most conservative paintings, her artistic integrity recoiled from this acclaimed but stodgy venue. At the same time, social dictates demanded that she marry. Appalled by the fate of her sister, who reluctantly set aside her paint brushes when she wed, Berthe held marriage at arms' length, enduring chaperones for every outing and remaining resignedly in her parents' home. Men unquestionably found her dark beauty attractive, but her talent and intelligence kept most suitors at bay. Until her eventual marriage, she seems to have had only one brush with romance—her encounters with the dashing artist Edouard Manet, a married man and womanizer who seemed fascinated by her, painting her almost a dozen times.

Berthe seems to have resisted Edouard, maintaining the quiet decorum that her milieu demanded. After all, affairs were not on the approved list for an unmarried woman of Paris' *haute bourgeoisie*. When, at the then-advanced age of thirty-three, she at last agreed to marry, her choice was Edouard Manet's quiet and gentle brother, Eugène—a nonartist with artistic sensibilities—who provided the kind of understanding and support she needed. Their wedding was small and simple, at the appealing neighborhood church of Notre-Dame de Grâce de Passy (10 Rue de l'Annonciation). Four years later, she gave birth to a daughter, Julie—a beautiful and intelligent child, whom both parents adored.

In the meantime, Berthe's career had exploded in unexpected directions. Invited to join Monet, Degas, Renoir, Pissarro, and Sisley at the first Impressionist Exhibition in 1874, she immediately became part of a small avant-garde that rocked the Paris art world. Accused by some of creating an art form so inherently vile that it threatened pregnant women and the social order, she suddenly found herself at the forefront of a revolution. That she was a woman made her role doubly revolutionary.

Her response to this kind of fame was typically measured. As a dedicated artist (one who had even chosen to take the then-unusual step of retaining her maiden, or professional, name), she was completely committed to her career, which was blossoming. Yet she retained the modesty and reticence of her upbringing—unlike the more forceful and publicity-minded American heiress and artist, Mary Cassatt, with whom Berthe always kept a cool reserve.

Instead, Berthe carefully maintained her privacy and propriety, carving out a rich life for herself and her family in Passy as well as in the hills of nearby Bougival—that virtual artist colony on the Seine, where she delighted in painting her family and garden. She also delighted in her friendships, and the Morisot-Manet summer residence on Bougival's winding Rue de la Princesse drew frequent visitors from Berthe's circle of Impressionist friends. Similarly, her soirées at 40 Rue de Villejust (now Rue Paul-Valéry), the gracious Morisot-Manet home near the Arc de Triomphe, became a center for artists, writers, and musicians.

Most of all, Berthe continued to paint. By this time she had exhibited at all but one of the Impressionists' subsequent exhibitions and had, like her colleagues, become established. And yet she remained dissatisfied with her work, continuing to strive toward that simple but elusive goal of capturing the transient on canvas.

Following Eugène's death (when she moved to a smaller place at 10 Rue Weber, adjoining her beloved Bois de Boulogne), she continued this search, painting Julie with ever quicker and looser brush strokes, as if to capture time itself. But time would not wait. Three years later, at the age of fifty-four, Berthe Morisot herself died.

Although Julie Manet did her best to perpetuate her mother's artistic legacy, Berthe Morisot soon slipped from public memory. In part, this may have been because she was a woman (both her marriage and death certificates astonishingly

Berthe Morisot medallion; 14 Quai de la Mégisserie

describe her as having "no profession"). But to at least some degree, Berthe Morisot's disappearance into history's shadows may reflect the modesty and propriety of her life.

Today you can find her tomb in Passy Cemetery, buried in classic simplicity with her husband Eugène and brother-in-law Edouard Manet. More importantly, you can find her works in the Musée d'Orsay (7th), the Musée Marmottan-Monet (16th), and the Musée du Petit Palais (8th), as well as in museums throughout the world.

Long relegated to the shadows, Berthe Morisot is at last beginning to receive the recognition she deserves.

26.

The Great Art Heist

AT 10:15 ON THE MORNING OF OCTOBER 27, 1985, FIVE gunmen entered the tranquil Musée Marmottan (16th) and made off with an armload of treasure—including Claude Monet's masterpiece, *Impression, Sunrise*, the painting that gave its name to the entire Impressionist Movement.

"A sacrilege!" exclaimed the Interior Ministry's appalled spokesman, who went on to compare this daring heist with the classic 1911 theft of Leonardo da Vinci's *Mona Lisa* from the venerable Louvre. Although the 20th century had seen more than its share of great art thefts, the greatest of them all—the touchstone for all truly serious art thieves—was unquestionably the removal of *La Joconde* from her sanctuary in the Louvre's Salon Carré.

An audacious theft—so much so that at first no one could believe it. Unlike the Monet heist, for a full day no one even realized the *Mona Lisa* was missing. Spirited away on a Monday morning, it was not until Tuesday that anyone thought to question where Leonardo's masterpiece might be. "Oh, the photographers have it," a guard replied, when an artist arrived to copy the famous Mona Lisa smile. The artist waited and waited, and then pressed again. Where was she? This time someone actually checked on her whereabouts, and now the authorities swung into action. More than one hundred policemen descended on the Louvre and locked the doors, searching the premises' forty-nine acres from top to bottom and questioning the hundreds of sightseers and employees still inside. Nothing turned up except the *Mona Lisa*'s frame, stashed in an inner staircase.

The work of a maniac, some concluded, or a discontented Louvre employee. Possibly even a blackmailer. But no leads or blackmail notes appeared, and in the frustrating days and weeks that followed, disconsolate Parisians lined the Salon Carré to stare at the empty space on the wall where their beloved painting had once hung.

An increasingly frantic Sûreté and Prefecture of Police tripped over each other in the effort to come up with something solid, and in their desperation lit upon a couple of unlikely suspects—the poet Guillaume Apollinaire and his friend, Pablo Picasso. Several years before, Apollinaire's friend and sometime secretary, Géry Pieret, had quietly lifted two ancient Iberian stone sculptures from the poorly guarded Louvre collections. Pieret promptly sold these to Picasso, who found inspiration there for his precedent-shattering Cubist work, *Les Demoiselles d'Avignon*. Indeed, if you look carefully at the painting's two central figures, you will see ears just like those of the stolen sculptures.

Both Pieret and Picasso regarded the matter as a joke, but Apollinaire thought otherwise. Alarmed, he tried to persuade Picasso to give the statues back, but with no luck. And then, after having left the city for several years, Pieret once again turned up—just as the *Mona Lisa* disappeared. Naturally, Apollinaire assumed that there was some connection between the two events, and soon the police reached the same conclusion. Terrified, Picasso returned the statues, incognito, while the police took Apollinaire into custody, on the assumption that the gentle poet was part of an international gang of art thieves. It took six hideous days in the Santé prison (still in operation on Rue de la Santé at Boulevard Arago, 14th) before the poet's friends managed to clear him and win his release.

Now the police were back to square one, chasing ephemeral leads for two dry years. Until, in 1913, the beloved painting unexpectedly came to light—in Italy. The thief, an Italian house painter by the name of Vincenzo Perugia, contacted a leading Florentine art dealer. Perugia requested money for living expenses, but claimed that his real motive was to return the *Mona Lisa* to the land of her birth. (He mistakenly thought that Napoléon had purloined it, when in fact François I had legitimately acquired her some four centuries earlier.)

Wrapped in red silk and carefully stowed in the false bottom of Perugia's battered trunk, the *Mona Lisa* emerged still smiling and none the worse for wear. All of France was ecstatic, especially when Italy agreed to return her to the Louvre. Perugia went to jail, but only briefly. After serving in the Italian army during World War I, he unaccountably returned to Paris, where he opened—what else?—a paint store.

How had he managed to steal the marvelous *Mona Lisa* in the first place? It had not been difficult, he told the judge. Not long before he stole *La Joconde*, the Louvre had decided to place her under glass. Perugia—who worked for the company given the contract—was one of four men assigned to the job. During that time, he had ample opportunity to see how the painting was hung. He also became known to a number of people on the Louvre staff, who saw nothing odd when he appeared several months later in his work smock, even though he was not in fact employed there at the time. Slipping into the Salon Carré early one Monday morning—cleaning day, when the Louvre was closed to the public—he waited until the guard disappeared from view, then unhooked the *Mona Lisa* from the wall and scurried down an interior staircase. There he removed the lady from her frame, stowed her beneath his smock, and left. Despite all the theories that had been whirling about, the *Mona Lisa* had spent her entire vacation in Perugia's humble Paris flat, at 5 Rue de l'Hôpital-Saint-Louis, 10th.

The 1985 Musée Marmottan theft was a very different, although equally dramatic affair. Perhaps paralleling the late-twentieth-century's taste for violence, the Marmottan's robbers made off with their paintings at gunpoint, brazenly entering the museum by day, when the alarm system was switched off. Coolly double-parking their car in front, two of the gunmen bought tickets and entered as visitors. Quickly locating what they wanted, they pulled out high-caliber revolvers and held nine unarmed museum guards and forty visitors at gunpoint, while three other thieves (who presumably had not purchased admission tickets) hastily pulled Impressionist masterpieces from the walls. In all, the hold-up—which closely resembled a bank robbery—lasted about five minutes.

Since all of the paintings were so well known and impossible to sell, experts concluded that this must be a "special-order theft," done for a reclusive private collector. When the years rolled by without any trace of the missing paintings, many assumed that they were lost forever.

That is, until 1987, when three stolen paintings from an earlier theft turned up in the hands of the Yakusa, or Japanese crime syndicate. Everything pointed to a similar Japanese connection in the Marmottan case, and soon the French police had their eye on the Corsican mob as well. Finally, in late 1990, the police dramatically discovered the missing paintings in an empty apartment in Porto Vecchio, Corsica.

Cleaned up and back where they belong, *Impression, Sunrise* and its companions once again have pride of place on the Marmottan's walls, just as the *Mona Lisa* has been contentedly smiling at throngs of Louvre visitors ever since her return in 1913. Not a bad adventure for a five hundred-year-old lady and her century-old colleagues, especially when all turned out so well.

X

ANOTHER REVOLUTION

From Laundry Boat to Beehive

NESTLED INTO QUIET NOOKS IN MONTMARTRE AND Montparnasse are two extraordinary structures with remarkable pasts. Although their renovated façades now convey an air of well-being, the strangely shaped Le Bateau-Lavoir (laundry boat) and La Ruche (beehive) once provided gritty and makeshift shelter for some of the most revolutionary artists of the twentieth century.

Being young and filled with new ideas, such artists were of course poor, and so the low-rent quarters that these ramshackle buildings provided had a definite appeal. Gravitating first to the rural slopes of Montmartre, which had only recently been joined to Paris following the destruction of the old tax wall, many ended up at the Bateau-Lavoir (13 Place Emile-Goudeau, 18th). This sprawling rabbit warren of a building, that spills three stories down the hill from Place Emile-Goudeau to Rue Garreau, served as a kind of headquarters for the constant flow of impoverished bohemians who worked, made love, argued endlessly, and caroused here during the building's glory years, from the 1890s to the outbreak of war in 1914.

At one point or another the Bateau-Lavoir's stream of inhabitants included the artists Utrillo, Brancusi, and Modigliani as well as the poet and painter Max Jacob, who took one look at the ungainly building and promptly christened it the Laundry Boat. Regular visitors included the artists Gauguin, Braque, and Matisse, while the painters van Dongen, Dufy, and Vlaminck made longer stays. Avant-garde poet Apollinaire was a regular, as were those American expatriates, Gertrude and Leo Stein. But of this entire star-studded bunch, the ringleader and superstar was Pablo Picasso.

Picasso arrived in 1904, at the age of twenty-three. His first address in Paris had been just down the street at 49 Rue Gabrielle. Devastated by the suicide of his friend, Carlos Casagemas, he made his way westward to Rue Ravignan, which curves into Place Emile-Goudeau (a recent name; in Picasso's day, the address was simply 13 Rue Ravignan). Settling into the Bateau-Lavoir, he found happiness in a tiny, filthy ground-floor studio unencumbered with gas, electricity, or indoor plumbing. Here, he met the beautiful young Fernande Olivier, who drew him out of his somber Blue Period. And here, in 1907, he crowned his stay with the path-breaking Cubist *Les Demoiselles d'Avignon*.

Picasso's arrival quickly transformed the place. With his huge eyes and intense gaze, he projected an allure that women found irresistible, while his compelling personality attracted a large group of male friends and associates. He and his band of friends soon gave the Bateau-Lavoir a certain cachet in artistic circles. When he departed, in 1909, the old Laundry Boat suddenly seemed far more drab.

Picasso left the Bateau-Lavoir simply because he had become successful. Although he departed reluctantly, he readily adapted to his clean and comfortable quarters (complete with maid) at nearby 11 Boulevard de Clichy. Others among his Bateau-Lavoir friends had also become successful and were moving on, but it was World War I that truly shattered the Laundry Boat's collective spirit. Some of its residents enlisted, some went to the front, and some died. When the survivors once again set up their easels at the war's end, it was this time in Montparnasse rather than in Montmartre.

Picasso himself gravitated to Montparnasse in 1912, following other artists who had already begun to settle here—including the impoverished residents of the Bateau-Lavoir's successor, La Ruche (15th). There in Passage de Dantzig, in the farthest reaches of Paris, painters and sculptors lived in total squalor as they reached for the stars. At La Ruche, Marc Chagall later recalled, "You either snuffed it or departed famous."

La Ruche was born in 1900, when Alfred Boucher, a successful society sculptor, bought a parcel of land at the southernmost edge of Paris, just inside the old fortifications and the present course of the Périphérique. There, downwind of a slaughterhouse and surrounded by a notorious wasteland, Boucher created an artists' colony. For his central building he acquired the stunning wine rotunda that Gustave Eiffel had designed for Paris' recently closed Universal Exposition. Divided into numerous small studios and surrounded by gardens, this remarkable octagonal edifice provided much-needed shelter for a pittance. Inaugurated as the Villa Médicis, the place quickly became known simply as La Ruche, or Beehive.

Constantly buzzing with activity, La Ruche became the home for the most starving of starving artists, many of whom came to Paris from Eastern Europe. Although the building itself was roofed in glass and its doorway splendidly supported by carved female figures, or caryatids, the interior apartments were cramped and without amenities, including heat. Boucher did his best to care for his unlikely family, charging virtually no rent and encouraging the revolutionary creativity going on beneath his oddly shaped roof. But anarchic and bohemian lifestyles did little to foster the clearly bourgeois promise of La Ruche's exterior, and most of the inhabitants of this unlikely oasis lived like bums.

La Ruche's heyday began around 1910, coinciding with the decline of the Bateau-Lavoir and the arrival of artists such as Chagall, Soutine, Archipenko, and Zadkine—founders of what became known as the Paris school. World War I disrupted this little artistic community, but it revived during the 1920s and 1930s, only to be almost annihilated during World War II, when the Gestapo dragged away Montparnasse's Jewish artists.

Both La Ruche and the Bateau-Lavoir soldiered on, but in

the following decades La Ruche was scheduled for destruction, and the Bateau-Lavoir burned to the ground (ironically, shortly after being declared an historic site). Fortunately, La Ruche has been saved and the Bateau-Lavoir has been rebuilt, much to the credit of those who have worked to preserve and restore these much-loved landmarks from Paris' cultural past.

Today, a leafy stillness prevails over both of these sites, once home to some of the most revolutionary and creative artists of the twentieth or any century. A cat prowls silently around the dappled courtyard of La Ruche, while a fountain trickles quietly beneath the chestnut trees in the Place Emile-Goudeau.

Both La Ruche and Le Bateau-Lavoir, rebuilt and restored to a state far better than they ever were during their prime, exude an air of well-being. The artists who have studios and live here are a well-heeled lot who fit easily into their now-respectable communities.

It would make Picasso and Chagall smile.

28.

Gertrude Stein and Company

In those heady years during the first decade or so of the twentieth century—the years that Max Jacob called the "heroic age of Cubism"—two of the trendiest addresses in town were the Bateau-Lavoir, on the slopes of Montmartre, and Gertrude Stein's art-filled atelier at 27 Rue de Fleurus (6ᵗʰ), near the Luxembourg Gardens. Between these humble residences a galaxy of Paris' avant-garde shuttled back and forth, including Gertrude Stein herself, who made the journey to Montmartre some eighty times just to pose for Pablo Picasso, who insisted that he could not get her portrait quite right. (Later, after finishing the masterpiece to his satisfaction, Picasso remarked that everyone said she did not look like that— but never mind, in time she would. And he was right.)

But while Picasso changed this feature and that, Gertrude Stein submitted with surprising meekness to his demands, returning again and again to his cluttered Bateau-Lavoir studio.

Not a small woman, Miss Stein (as she referred to herself) found the uphill climb grueling. Still, she was sufficiently convinced of young Picasso's genius that she regularly tramped across the Luxembourg Gardens to Place de l'Odéon, where she boarded a horse-drawn omnibus to the foot of Montmartre. Debarking at the Moulin Rouge, she climbed steep Rue Lepic (which is still, as she then noted, "lined with shops with things to eat") to Rue Ravignan and the Bateau-Lavoir. Then, after posing for Picasso, she walked back down the Butte and all the way home—undoubtedly acquiring a pastry en route.

It was a pleasant and scintillating life, one enlivened by countless visitors at her own famous address. This small *pavillon*, or detached house, adjoined a garden courtyard and large atelier. Here in the atelier, Miss Stein hung the numerous—and increasingly valuable—works of contemporary art that she and her brother, Leo, began to purchase almost immediately upon arriving in Paris, in 1903. It was a fabulous and eclectic collection, but no more so than the guests who congregated there.

Among the regulars were Picasso and his mistress, the beautiful Fernande Olivier. Another was Henri Matisse—until he made the mistake of asking what was for dinner before deciding to stay. During these early days, the poet Guillaume Apollinaire was also an habitué, along with

Caricature of Gertrude Stein after Picasso

his mistress, the artist Marie Laurencin. And then there was the painter, Henri Rousseau.

Sweetly vague and naively original, Rousseau painted so astonishingly that even the members of the wildly experimental Montmartre set were hard pressed to know what to make of him. At length, in tribute to Rousseau's originality if not to his still-unrecognized genius, Picasso decided to throw a banquet for the fellow. Always game for a party, the rest of the crowd fell in, including Miss Stein and her inseparable companion, Alice B. Toklas.

As usual for this uninhibited crowd, something went wildly wrong. The caterer developed second thoughts and didn't show up, but no one minded. Everyone had come for the booze and a good time, and by early evening, as they congregated in the little café at the foot of Rue Ravignan, a spirit of riotous good cheer rapidly developed. At last they set out for the Bateau-Lavoir, with Miss Stein supporting a very drunk Marie Laurencin the entire way. Fernande—who had never liked Marie Laurencin—took one look at the swaying young woman and demanded that she leave, but Miss Stein was adamant. Not after all the work of getting her up that hill. Marie Laurencin stayed, but the disasters continued, culminating in Apollinaire's very drunk brother eating the gorgeous yellow flower off of Alice B. Toklas' beloved new hat.

A memorable evening—one that went down in Montmartre history. But already success was making inroads on these youthful revelries, and before long the old gang—most notably Picasso and Fernande—split up and moved on. Picasso now moved to Montparnasse, at 5 bis Rue Victor-Schoelcher (14th), not far from Gertrude Stein. Since many others in Miss Stein's circle also lived nearby, there now was much traipsing back and forth along Boulevard Raspail (so cold in winter that the friends referred to it as the "retreat from Moscow").

Picasso retained an ongoing although frequently bumpy friendship with Miss Stein, even as his friendship with Matisse chilled into intense rivalry. Given the colossal egos involved— not least of all that of Gertrude Stein herself—it was perhaps a wonder that any of them ever got along at all.

Ernest Hemingway was quick to observe this when he met Miss Stein in the early 1920s. By this time she had begun to make her mark as a highly unconventional writer, while her reputation as a collector and hostess continued to grow. Adding to old friends and replacing those who had drifted away, she turned to a new genera- tion of writers and artists, including members of the expatriate community. Indeed, it was Gertrude Stein who famously called the post–World War I expatriates the "Lost Generation."

Hemingway first met her in the Luxembourg Gardens, where he frequently walked to escape the confines of his small apartment (at 74 Rue du Cardinal-Lemoine) and office (at 39 Rue Descartes), both just off Place de la Contrescarpe, 5th. Looking quite like the Italian peasant that Picasso had long before painted, Miss Stein invited Hemingway to come by any time after 5:00 P.M.

There at 27 Rue de Fleurus, young Hemingway admired the paintings, enjoyed the liqueurs, and—like so many before him— became engrossed in his hostess' conversation. But there he also became aware of the huge personality that she exercised over her guests, either to charm or to overwhelm. As someone possessing no small amount of personality and charm himself, he found that his admiration for this living legend eventually waned. He parted, giving a very different account of their falling-out than did Miss Stein—who enjoyed backstabbing him in the company of his rival, Sherwood Anderson.

Other failed friendships littered Gertrude Stein's social landscape, including Sylvia Beach, founder of the original Shakespeare and Company (at 12 Rue de l'Odéon, 6ᵗʰ). Beach published James Joyce's *Ulysses*—a seismic event in literary history, but a book that so seriously offended Miss Stein that the two parted ways.

The soirées at 27 Rue de Fleurus continued, with new friends and acquaintances replacing the old. By the late 1930s, when Gertrude Stein moved from her Montparnasse salon to an apartment on Rue Christine (6ᵗʰ), even the choice of paintings in her famed atrium had significantly changed. A predominance of Picassos and Cézannes now replaced the original layout. (Matisse seemed to disappear from her walls as well as from her salon.)

An era was over—all the more so with Miss Stein's death in 1946. But it is still possible to walk past 27 Rue de Fleurus and peer through the glassed gates to the garden courtyard behind. Here, for almost forty years, Gertrude Stein worked to change the literary landscape. And here, this indomitable American surrounded herself with like-minded adventurers—some of the most remarkable writers and artists in the world.

NOTE: Picasso's famous portrait of Gertrude Stein now hangs in the Metropolitan Museum of Art in New York.

29.
A Sculptor's Muse

"Mademoiselle," Aristide Maillol wrote fifteen-year-old Dina Vierny in 1934, "I am told that you resemble a Maillol or a Renoir. I would be satisfied with a Renoir."

As it happened, Vierny had exactly the voluptuous figure that Maillol had idealized and sculpted for years, and their collaboration during the last decade of his life prompted a brilliant resurgence in his career.

Maillol had not always been a sculptor. Born in the south of France in 1861, he moved to Paris at twenty to become a painter, eventually trying his hand at ceramics and tapestry design as well. Only after the turn of the century did he turn full-time to sculpture, with remarkable results. Breaking with the passionate expressionism of Rodin and other late-nineteenth-century French sculptors, he astonished the art world with a series of serene, almost abstract, female nudes—expressionless or even headless creatures whose smooth, sensual roundness and classical restraint revolutionized twentieth-century sculpture.

From the outset, Maillol set out to express powerful yet abstract ideas through the human form, especially through an idealized vision of the perfect female figure. Vierny most happily turned out to be a flesh-and-blood realization of his ideal. Buxom and scarcely more than five feet tall, Vierny may not have been the twenty-first century's idea of perfection, but Maillol was enchanted with her. Nor was he alone, for she also modeled for artists such as Pierre Bonnard, Raoul Dufy, and Henri Matisse.

Unquestionably beautiful, Vierny proved courageous as well. During the German Occupation, she risked her life by helping Jews escape from France. After the war and Maillol's death, she showed this same spirit in establishing her own Paris art gallery, promoting Maillol and other contemporary artists she deemed worthy of public attention.

Intelligent, discerning, and bold, she searched out and showed a wide range of cutting-edge art, including French primitivists and members of Russia's postwar avant-garde. She also collected works by Kandinsky and Poliakoff, as well as by Degas, Bonnard, Matisse, Gaugin, and Cézanne.

Early on, as she was building both her gallery and private collection, she made a magnificent gift of Maillol sculptures to the Tuileries Gardens. (They are now located in the adjacent Jardin du Carrousel.) This was just a start, for she had already decided to establish a museum that would exhibit the full range of Maillol's work, in addition to displaying her own collection. Tenacious and persevering, she acquired a remarkable eighteenth-century *hôtel particulier* in the Faubourg Saint-Germain and set out to refurbish it.

At last, in 1995, Vierny—and her Fondation Dina Vierny—opened the Musée Maillol in the Hôtel Bouchardon (59-61 Rue de Grenelle, 7th). Built over an ancient convent, this striking edifice contains Edme Bouchardon's sculpted *Fountain of the Four Seasons*, which is the focal point of the mansion's graceful semicircular façade. Inside, a well-designed restoration highlighted by beamed ceilings and a spiral staircase provides an intimate yet airy setting for the remarkable collection that Vierny has opened to the public.

Here you will find a treasure-trove of twentieth-century art, including some deliberately provocative entries by the Duchamp brothers and a somber example of installation art by Ilya Kabakov. But the starring attraction is always Maillol, from his paintings, drawings, ceramics, and tapestries to his most monumental sculptures, including *La Rivière*.

In opening this exceptional collection to the public, Dina Vierny—model and sculptor's muse—has preserved Aristide Maillol's legacy for the ages. Maillol certainly could not have asked, or hoped, for more.

XI

RESISTANCE

The Few and the Daring

UP AGAINST THE EASTERN WALL OF THE MOAT
surrounding the Château de Vincennes, at the edge of Paris,
stands a white wooden cross emblazoned with the colors of
France. Take a moment to gaze at it in respectful silence, for
here, in August 1944—during the last days of the German
Occupation—some thirty members of the French Resistance
died at the hands of a Nazi firing squad.

Nowhere was it riskier for the Resistance to operate than in
Occupied Paris, where the chances of arrest were exceptionally
high. Parisians, of course, had a formidable reputation for
resisting oppression, but when the Germans marched into the
City of Light in June 1940, they so overwhelmed its citizens
with their military might and intelligence apparatus that they
quickly and effectively took control.

In a dispiriting show of swastikas and leather jackboots, the
German occupying forces selected the best parts of town for

their headquarters, requisitioning so many buildings in the 16th arrondissement that it was a wonder some of its fashionable streets did not sink under their weight. While top military brass were quartered at the Hotel Majestic, just south of the Arc de Triomphe, the SS, Gestapo, and security police swarmed into a number of fine buildings near the Bois de Boulogne.

The most notorious addresses of all were 82-84 Avenue Foch (headquarters of the Bureau for Locating and Repressing the Resistance) and 11 Rue des Saussaies, 8th—which was widely regarded as Gestapo headquarters. In both locations, Resistance suspects were routinely interrogated, tortured, and killed. In *The World at Night*, novelist Alan Furst's protagonist escapes from a basement cell in 11 Rue des Saussaies, but this is a story. In actuality, the only dependable way out was death, and a striking number of arrested Resistance members killed themselves to avoid torture and to keep from betraying comrades and secrets.

Given the overwhelming odds, it's hardly surprising that the Resistance movement in Paris got off to a slow start. Even though General de Gaulle stirringly proclaimed (via a BBC broadcast from London) that "the flames of Resistance must not extinguish and will not extinguish," it was difficult to make headway in a city where everyone was so closely watched. One of de Gaulle's supporters, Maurice Duclos, soon learned what he was up against when, in late 1940, he began to set up a Paris network covering western France. Breaking a leg as he parachuted in from London, Duclos was first betrayed by his doctor. Managing to escape, he next was betrayed by his Paris radio operator. With ruthless precision, the Gestapo then rolled up most of his fledgling network.

Still, a growing number of Parisians were beginning to defy the Occupation. Using hit-and-run tactics, they threw grenades and fired on the enemy, keeping up the harassment even when the Germans took to executing hostages in reprisal.

Despite such daring exploits, there was as yet little coordination or even cooperation among the various components of what would become the French Resistance. No one was yet in charge, although there were plenty of leaders—including Pierre Brossolette, the heroic left-wing journalist and broadcaster. Adamantly anti-Fascist, Brossolette daringly operated right under the noses of the Gestapo, out of a bookstore he bought at 89 Rue de la Pompe, in the 16th arrondissement. Although by then living on the Left Bank, at 123 Rue de Grenelle (7th), Brossolette knew this part of the 16th well, having attended school right across the street. A touching plaque on the school wall reminds the passerby not to forget Brossolette's extraordinary heroism in the face of the "upsurge of barbarism in Europe."

At 89 Rue de la Pompe (also marked by a plaque), Brossolette and other members of his network published a clandestine anti-Fascist newspaper until the group's arrest in early 1941. Seven of the network's twenty-four members were executed at Mont Valérien—a nineteenth-century fortress overlooking western Paris that had already become notorious for its Nazi-run prison and firing squad. Brossolette, who remained free, courageously continued to work with Resistance leaders in Paris and northern France before heading to London—one step ahead of the Nazis—to join de Gaulle's Free French government in exile.

There he stayed long enough to become a high-ranking member of de Gaulle's intelligence service, and then parachuted back into France with two other Resistance legends—de Gaulle's chief of intelligence, André Dewavrin (alias Colonel Passy), and British intelligence's F. F. E. Yeo-Thomas. Spirited away to safe houses, they met with leaders of the major Resistance groups, planning strategy and working to create a unified underground force under de Gaulle's leadership.

De Gaulle's choice to head the united Resistance effort was Jean Moulin, a remarkable administrator and dynamic leader with strong anti-Fascist convictions. Although he had risen rapidly through the prewar civil service to become France's youngest prefect, the collaborationist Vichy government quickly dismissed him when he strenuously objected to Nazi atrocities and refused to participate in a cover-up. The Germans arrested and tortured him, but could not force him to recant. To prevent capitulation and dishonor, Moulin slashed his throat with a piece of broken glass. Surprisingly, he recovered. Not so surprisingly, the Vichy government tried to cover up the entire affair.

Moulin was now well on his way toward a leading role in the Resistance. Casting his lot with de Gaulle, who entrusted him with the mission of unifying and leading the movement, he worked throughout 1942 and early 1943 to smooth out differences among the hot-headed, stubborn, and utterly committed individuals who held out for their own particular strategies and organizations. At last, in 1943, he succeeded in creating the National Council of the Resistance, uniting the entire Resistance under de Gaulle, with himself as president. It was a heady moment when the Council stealthily held its first meeting on May 27, 1943, at 48 Rue du Four (6th), with representatives of all the leading Resistance organizations in attendance.

Contrary to some reports, the apartment did not belong to Moulin, who would have risked his own life as well as everyone else's by such a choice. Instead, he chose the apartment of a friend for this unprecedented meeting, while he himself lived anonymously in the heart of the 14th arrondissement, at 26 Rue des Plantes (not far from the street that has since been renamed Avenue Jean-Moulin). By now, he was the most wanted man in France and had to assume that he was living in death's shadow. Indeed, only three months before, the Nazis had captured and shot his friend, Lucien Legros, as well as four other student Resistance fighters. A large medallion at the southern end of the Gare Montparnasse (15th), at the Place des Cinq-Martyrs-du-Lycée-Buffon, commemorates these students' heroism.

The Gestapo—specifically, Klaus Barbie—finally caught up with Moulin in June 1943, probably after a betrayal. Once again, Moulin remained cool under brutal torture, at one point simply drawing a cartoon of his interrogator when handed a pad of paper on which to confess. He died in July, at the hands of the Gestapo, having remained silent to the end. Unquestionably one of France's greatest heroes, he is now buried in the Panthéon.

Following Moulin's death, Brossolette returned to France to help lead the movement, and soon fell into Nazi hands. Emile Bollaert, another of de Gaulle's handpicked leaders of the Resistance, was arrested with him. Apparently unaware of Bollaert's true identity, the Germans sent him to Bergen-Belsen, where he managed to survive until the British liberated the death camp in 1945. He then returned to France and served it well for fifteen years, dying peacefully in 1978.

Pierre Brossolette was not so lucky. Someone tipped off the Germans, and soon he was taken to 84 Avenue Foch. When tortured, he did not talk, but must have agonized that he might. On March 22, 1944, he slipped past his guards and hurled himself out a fifth-floor window. He died soon after and was cremated at Père-Lachaise Cemetery (20th). In a final indignity, his remains (#3920 in the Columbarium) are labeled "Inconnu Incinéré, 24-3-44." The cemetery map gives a name to these otherwise nameless ashes, but many other cremated bodies in Père-Lachaise, dating from the German Occupation, remain unidentified—an unsettling reminder of the darkness and terror of those years.

There are other reminders throughout Paris, if you take the time to look. The Square de la Roquette (11th), not far from Père-Lachaise's western entrance, is now an attractive garden with a pleasant fountain. But take a close look at the park's gate (at 147 Rue de la Roquette). It's scary, and rightly so, for this was once the entrance to a horrendous prison. As you look at those barred windows, remember that during the long years of Occupation, some four thousand Resistance fighters were imprisoned here. A plaque, all too easily over-looked, reminds the passerby that these prisoners "contributed to the Liberation of France."

Similarly, Picpus Cemetery, hidden (at 35 Rue de Picpus, 12th) in a residential area just south of the Place de la Nation, presents a peaceful face to the world. But here lie not only the many aristocratic victims of Place de la Nation's Revolutionary guillotine, but also their descendants, including a number who joined in the Resistance to the German Occupation. If you decide to visit, be sure to pick an afternoon between 2:00 and 4:00 P.M. (closed Monday).

Père-Lachaise, of course, has a memorial (in division 97) for those Resistance fighters who were executed, as well as stirring tributes to those who died in Nazi concentration camps or in fighting the Fascists in Spain. These are a powerful and moving group of monuments, well worth the long walk to the cemetery's southeast corner.

There are streets and parks all over Paris dedicated to fallen and otherwise little-known members of the Resistance. Square René-le-Gall, in the 13th, commemorates a government official shot by the Germans, while Square Suzanne-Buisson, a restful children's playground high on Montmartre (Avenue Junot, 18th), is dedicated to the memory of one of the many women who fought the Occupation and died for France. The Place de la Résistance, at Pont de l'Alma in the 7th, is dedicated to all who fought the German Occupation.

Just a short distance away, near the Pont de Bir-Hakeim (15th), is the site of the infamous Vélodrome d'Hiver, or Vél d'Hiv, a covered cycling arena that the Nazis used as a staging area for the death camps. Here, starting on July 16, 1942, the police rounded up thousands of Jewish men, women, and children, cramming them together under ghastly conditions before deporting them to the camps. The Vél d'Hiv has been demolished, but the Place des Martyrs-Juifs-du-Vélodrome-d'Hiver now commemorates this atrocity. Each year an annual ceremony pays tribute to the suffering of wartime Paris Jews and the horrors that took place here.

Farther up the Seine, at the eastern tip of the Ile de la Cité, the stark Memorial of the Deportation pays solemn tribute to those many thousands of deportees to the death camps, while almost directly across the Seine, an eternal flame burns at the Memorial to the Unknown Jewish Martyr. This, along with extensive archives and the Mur des Noms (Wall of Names) recording the seventy-six thousand French victims of the Holocaust, is located in the Mémorial de la Shoah, in the heart of the Right Bank's old Jewish Quarter (17 Rue Geoffroy-l'Asnier, 4th).

Less accessible but well worth a visit is the Musée Jean-Moulin, a fascinating museum on the Resistance located at the northern end of the Jardin Atlantique, on the roof of the Gare Montparnasse (15th)—not far from the Place des Cinq-Martyrs-du-Lycée-Buffon. Linked with another small museum commemorating the Liberation of Paris (Mémorial du Maréchal Leclerc de Hauteclocque et de la Libération de Paris), the Musée Jean-Moulin provides a well-organized introduction to the major themes and players of the Resistance, most

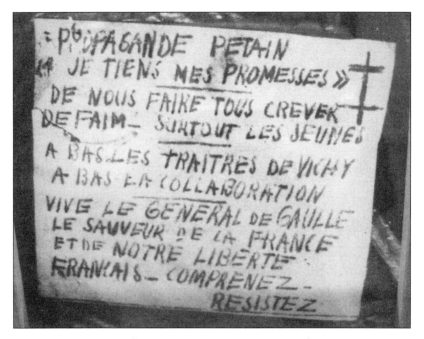

Handwritten protest, Musée Jean-Moulin

especially Moulin himself. Here you will find videotaped interviews with Resistance survivors, along with a wealth of other material, including posters and publications, with good explanatory notes in English as well as in French.

By linking the two museums—one on the Resistance and the other on the Liberation—the City of Paris underscores the Resistance's basic purpose: to liberate Paris, and all of France, from Nazi Occupation. Upstairs, a 360-degree projection of actual news footage from the Liberation of Paris provides a vivid illustration of this point, placing you right in the center of some of the action—including an unforgettable gun battle practically on the steps of Notre-Dame.

Throughout the long years leading to this extraordinary moment, Moulin had worked not only to unify the Resistance, but also to keep its most hotheaded leaders from triggering a premature uprising. Any such action taken without full Allied military support, Moulin argued, would be futile—and would allow the Germans to destroy the entire Resistance movement. Wait for the Allies to land, he urged. Wait.

In the end, the Resistance leaders waited. Throughout the long years from the fall of France in 1940 to the Normandy invasion in 1944, they set up their networks, collected intelligence, spread propaganda, smuggled out downed Allied pilots, and conducted sabotage as well as guerrilla warfare. They lived in a world of shadows, a world of danger, in which death could be—and often was—just around the corner.

"Like thousands of other French citizens, I accepted the idea of death from the very outset of the war," Jean Moulin wrote in his diary in early 1941. "I am not afraid of it." A grim but realistic assessment. The Nazis deported between sixty thousand and sixty-five thousand Resistance members to death camps, where barely half survived. And the Nazis executed thousands more. At Mont Valérien, they marched prisoners in groups to a small clearing, where a firing squad awaited them. In all, some one thousand prisoners died in this single spot. (There is now a massive France in Combat war memorial near the place where these executions took place, at Fort Mont Valérien in Suresnes.)

Paris now commemorates this extraordinary heroism and sacrifice every November 11 (Armistice Day), placing fresh flowers on each Parisian plaque and memorial commemorating the Resistance and those who have "died for France." Look for these floral tributes if you are in Paris on that day. Blue, white, and red, with a tricolor ribbon, they bring tears to one's eyes. Take a moment to gaze in silence, for here a French citizen—most likely a Parisian—paid the ultimate price for liberty.

XII

PEACE on EARTH

31.

In Zadkine's Garden

THINKING BACK ACROSS THE YEARS, I DISTINCTLY remember a photograph my parents took in Rotterdam not long after World War II. There in this picture loomed a huge bronze figure, its arms outstretched in anguish, its torso pierced with a jagged hole—much as Rotterdam itself had suffered after Germany bombed its heart out.

Many times I have thought of this sculpture. And then, not long ago, I was delighted—and a bit startled—to come upon a smaller version of it in Paris.

I had found my way into the garden of the Musée Zadkine, the former home and studio of the sculptor Ossip Zadkine. One of a flood of artists from Russia and Central Europe who arrived in Paris during the heady years before World War I, he first washed up—along with so many of his fellows in what became known as the Paris school—at the fabled La Ruche. He should have fit in well here with compatriots such as Chagall,

Soutine, and Lipchitz, but he hated La Ruche, finding nothing either pleasant or romantic about its living conditions or even its legendary bonhomie.

Fortunately, he did not have to stay long. Escaping after only six months, he briefly used a studio at 114 Rue de Vaugirard and then moved on to 35 Rue Rousselet. But no residence in Paris truly pleased him until, in 1928, he bought a rustic house and garden at the end of a small lane behind Rue d'Assas (100 bis, Rue d'Assas, 6th), near the Luxembourg Gardens. "Come see my pleasure house," he wrote a friend, "and you'll understand how much a man's life can be changed by a dovecote, by a tree."

This comment may at first seem baffling, for although Zadkine's new-found dovecote and trees provided him with idyllic working conditions, they did not inspire him to celebrate either beauty or nature—at least, not in any traditional sense. In fact, having survived a Jewish boyhood under the Russian Empire, as well as front-line service during World War I, where he served as a stretcher-bearer, Zadkine retained a particularly dark vision of the world around him. Yet, always a humanist, he found in this tranquil setting the inspiration and freedom he needed to channel his anguish over the human condition into ever more powerful and dramatic forms.

Having found a measure of peace in his Paris studio and garden, he remained there until his death in 1967, evolving during the course of a long career from Primitivism and Cubism to the highly individual and abstract style of his later years. Only during the German Occupation did he temporarily escape to New York, returning immediately after the war to Rue d'Assas, where he produced some of his finest sculptures—including his famous Rotterdam memorial, which many consider his masterpiece.

Thanks to a Parisian acquaintance who put the Musée Zadkine on her list of "musts," I recently made my way into the museum's garden, where I found the model for this very masterpiece. The day was rainy, but it didn't matter. I had already wandered through the museum's five rooms, where some of Zadkine's most important works are displayed (thanks to a bequest to the City of Paris by Zadkine's wife, the painter Valentine Prax). And then I sampled the diminutive garden. There by the front gate stood the sculpture of my memories.

I stood silently for several moments. And then I took a picture for my parents.

Nagasaki Angel

PRECISELY AT 8:15 A.M. ON A HOT AND SUNNY AUGUST 6, 1945, a B-29 Superfortress with the unlikely name of Enola Gay unleashed its atomic cargo on Hiroshima, leveling the city and killing 130,000 people. Three days later, another Superfortress dropped an even more powerful atomic bomb ("Fat Man") on Nagasaki, instantly vaporizing it.

In the town of Urakami, on Nagasaki's outskirts, the largest Roman Catholic church in Japan collapsed into a pile of scorched rubble, crushing Father Saburo Nishida and numerous parishioners inside. It had taken thirty years to build this Romanesque-style cathedral in Urakami, a town where Christianity (introduced by Portuguese traders) had thrived for centuries, even during periods of persecution. By the time "Fat Man" annihilated it, the Urakami cathedral had become one of the largest Christian churches in the Far East.

Now this beloved church was totally destroyed. But as the

devastated survivors combed their church's ruins, they found an unexpected ray of hope—a fragment of a sculpted angel that had miraculously survived. Her torso had crumbled into dust, but her head and wings remained intact. Even her lovely face was still recognizable, although the bomb's blast had marred one of her eyes, making her appear—on first glimpse—as if she had been crying.

This treasure, known as the Nagasaki Angel, now is sheltered at the Paris headquarters of UNESCO, the United Nations Educational, Scientific and Cultural Organization. In 1976 the town of Nagasaki parted with her, to honor UNESCO in its thirtieth anniversary year.

Nagasaki's gift was both deeply moving and extraordinarily fitting, for since its inception UNESCO has dedicated itself to promoting international peace. UNESCO's headquarters, located at 7 Place de Fontenoy (7th), near the Eiffel Tower, is itself a tribute to international artistic cooperation. The unusual Y-shaped Secretariat and its two smaller accompanying buildings are the product of three archi-

Nagasaki Angel, UNESCO

tects (French, Italian, and American), while some of the leading artists of the twentieth century contributed to the buildings' decor.

Pablo Picasso, an impassioned opponent of war, contributed a huge mural *(The Fall of Icarus)*, while his fellow Spaniard, Joan Miró, created stunning ceramic decorations *(Wall of the Sun* and *Wall of the Moon)*. Near Picasso's mural you will find a tapestry by French architect and artist Le Corbusier, while a walk in the piazza to the west yields a wealth of fine art, including sculptures by Henry Moore (British), Alexander Calder (American), and Alberto Giacometti (Swiss).

But it is the beautiful garden to the east that provides the most touching tributes to peace, including the Nagasaki Angel herself. Here, in utter tranquility, a Japanese water garden adjoins a Square of Tolerance, dedicated to slain Israeli prime minister Yitzhak Rabin.

The small Square of Tolerance, with its thought-provoking olive tree, offers a quiet place for meditation, but it is the Japanese Garden of Peace that truly refreshes the soul. Here, in this small masterpiece by Isamu Noguchi, water cascades, ripples, falls, drips, or lies completely tranquil in small ponds carefully dotted with water lilies and perfectly placed stepping stones. Follow a succession of walkways and bridges to the garden's far end, where a mosaic mural by Jean Bazaine *(Water Rhythm)* continues the theme.

Then return to the top of the garden and its Fountain of Peace. For it is here, nestled against a wall, that you will find the tiny Nagasaki Angel in all her tender beauty. A more poignant and powerful plea for Peace on Earth is difficult to imagine.

33.

A University for Peace

THE 1920S WERE NOT JUST ABOUT FLAPPERS, FIZZING champagne bottles, and all that jazz. Although undoubtedly an age of frivolity, frothing up in the wake of World War I, this delightful and decadent era also saw a remarkable rise in idealism on the diplomatic front, including the League of Nations and Woodrow Wilson's famed vision of a world made safe for democracy. It was in this environment that a remarkable experiment in international living got its start.

It began when a wealthy French industrialist by the name of Emile Deutsch de la Meurthe decided that he wanted to create some sort of tangible legacy. He contacted Paul Appell, Rector of the University of Paris, who at that moment was despairing over the postwar dearth of student housing. Together with André Honnorat, Minister of Public Instruction, the three came up with the idea of a *cité universitaire*, or campus of residence halls—not a novel idea in itself, except that this particular group of residence halls would have a unique and heartfelt purpose. True to the spirit of the times, the Cité Internationale Universitaire de Paris would be dedicated to promoting international peace.

The idea was that if enough students from the four corners of the world lived together in close quarters, they would form friendships and learn to understand and appreciate one another. Walls of bigotry and misunderstanding would crumble, and wars like the terrible one from which they had all just emerged would never again happen. In this spirit, the first buildings of this experiment—the gabled houses of the Fondation Emile et Louise Deutsch de La Meurthe—opened in 1925. Perhaps significantly, the land provided for this endeavor was an eighty-five-acre strip, deep in the 14th arrondissement, that became available at the end of World War I when the last outmoded fortifications surrounding Paris were torn down.

Other buildings on this international residential campus quickly followed, thanks to generous support from numerous governments, corporations, and private individuals. Within a dozen years, nineteen more houses went up, including International House, the gift of John D. Rockefeller, Jr. Although all building stopped during and immediately following World War II, it once again resumed in the 1950s, with Africa now represented. Between 1950 and 1969, when the last house was completed, seventeen others joined the previous twenty.

Today, the Cité Internationale houses some 5,500 students from more than 130 countries. The majority of them live with others of their own nationality (Americans, for example, in the Fondation des Etats-Unis, and Japanese in the Maison du Japon)—an arrangement that had its origins in the clubbier 1920s but now appears curiously contradictory to the Cité's basic purpose. In response to this potential clannishness, the various houses now reserve at least a third of their rooms for students from other countries, and consciously mix their residents, in the hope of encouraging international contacts. In addition, students mingle in the campus restaurants, library, theater, orchestra, chorus, team competitions, and sports facilities.

Although the original concept of national houses may be outmoded, the resulting architecture is always interesting and sometimes striking. Whatever the current status of your academic aspirations, the Cité Internationale campus is well worth a visit. Located on a landscaped park along Boulevard Jourdan (14th), across from Parc Montsouris and the RER, the Cité Internationale is a kind of world's fair of architecture—and a good place for a stroll.

Begin your exploration at the main entrance, at 19 Boulevard Jourdan. Here you will be greeted by International House, a château-style building in the tradition of Louis XIII, directly inspired by the château of Fontainebleau. Housing the main restaurant, quarters for visiting professors, library, swimming pool, theater, and other student services, this clearly is the visual and functional focal point of the entire campus.

From here, wandering to the east, you will pass the United States entry (solid and impressive, but not an architectural standout) and the extravagantly turreted and gabled Fondation

Biermans-Lapôtre, representing Belgium and Luxembourg. Other buildings of interest along this stretch include Japan House, looking a bit like a Nipponese temple, and Brazil House, a frankly aggressive piece of architecture designed by Lucio Costa in conjunction with the famed French architect Le Corbusier. But the prize of this section, and of the entire campus, is Le Corbusier's 1932 Swiss House, a clean-lined and airborne structure that is open on its ground level, resting its entire weight on a mere set of elongated pillars or piles.

As you cross to the western portion of the campus, look back at the Fondation Avicenne (originally Iran House)—a remarkable architectural statement by French architect Claude Parent. The most recent of all the Cité Internationale buildings (1968), this entire structure is daringly suspended from a huge metal framework.

Returning across wooded areas and playing fields, be sure to catch a glimpse of the original campus, the seven-building Deutsch de la Meurthe group, reminiscent of Oxford or Cambridge. Beyond that, the fresco adorning the entry of the Résidence Lucien Paye (originally founded for students from French colonial Africa) is eye-catching, as is the pillared entrance to the Greek House. At the far end you will undoubtedly notice the striking South-East Asia House (formerly Indochina's house), but don't overlook the more quietly imposing Dutch Hall (Collège Néerlandais), a 1930s gem designed by Willem Marinus Dubok.

The concept of promoting international understanding in such a fashion proved a popular one. Cité Internationale is now linked with thirteen other student International Houses around the globe, including five in the United States alone (New York, Chicago, Philadelphia, Washington, D.C., and Berkeley). There are also International Houses in Japan, Taiwan, the United Kingdom, and Australia. Of these, the Paris campus is still by far the most ambitious.

Of course, its aging designer buildings require constant upkeep and care. Yet three-quarters of a century after its founding, the Cité Internationale Universitaire de Paris is still going strong—actively promoting its vision for a better and more peaceful world.

XIII

JAZZ AGE

34.

American Princess

WINNARETTA SINGER WAS NOT BEAUTIFUL—EVERYONE agreed on that. But she was intelligent, sensitive, and gifted. Best of all, she was rich, and in time this wealthy and cultivated young woman would become not only a talented musician and artist in her own right, but one of the foremost patrons of the arts in Paris.

Her origins were almost as unusual as her name. Her father, Isaac Merritt Singer, had made a fortune through his invention of the sewing machine, but in his youth had fancied himself an actor, turning to work as a machinist only to keep from starving. A romantic and impractical soul, he lived with a series of mistresses who, over the years, bore him a total of sixteen illegitimate children. In turn, the Frenchwoman he eventually married—and who became Winnaretta's mother—proceeded to bear him six more.

Winnaretta, the second of Isaac's legitimate family, owed her name to her father, who probably invented it. But she owed her love of music to her mother, the beautiful young Isabelle Boyer, who used the Singer fortune to further her social ambitions and to surround herself with music.

You can still see the two Paris houses in which Winnaretta grew up, the first at 83 bis Boulevard Malesherbes (8th), near the Parc Monceau, and the second at 27 Avenue Kléber (16th), in the shadow of the Arc de Triomphe.

Isaac Singer died in 1875, when Winnaretta was only ten, leaving her a hefty fortune and a mother who was far more concerned with her own social triumphs than she was with her shy and awkward daughter. The beautiful Madame Singer quickly remarried, this time acquiring a title.

Winnaretta, who had neither her mother's beauty nor social ambition, keenly felt her mother's disappointment in her, but found refuge in the arts. As a teenager, she studied painting and had established herself as a promising artist by the time she was twenty. She was also a talented organist. But her personal life continued to be painful, exacerbated by her mother's self-absorption as well as by Winnaretta's growing awareness of her own lesbianism.

Marriage under such circumstances, even to escape the family home, offered little in the way of a solution, and Winnaretta's first marriage proved disastrous. But a second marriage, to Prince Edmond de Polignac, turned out extremely well, discreetly accommodating both partners' sexual preferences while providing an affectionate and last-ing companionship. The two, who met in a bidding war over a Monet painting, shared a deep love for art and music, and under their auspices the Hôtel de Polignac became one of the foremost salons in turn-of-the-century Paris.

Winnaretta bought this lovely mansion, which still stands at 43 Avenue Georges-Mandel (16th), at the same time that the starkly futuristic Eiffel Tower was going up directly across the Seine. Some might have considered the controversial tower a daunting neighbor, but Winnaretta embraced the new with enthusiasm, and her salon—held in the mirrored music room overlooking a quiet side street—introduced a select group of Parisians to some of the most contemporary and challenging music of the day.

During the years that Princess Winnaretta held sway, from the 1890s through the 1930s, Paris' vibrant cultural scene included names such as Debussy, Ravel, Fauré, and Proust. Winnaretta knew and quietly encouraged all of these, plus many more, providing moral support, financial help, and a showcase for their work in her own salon.

The Polignac *soirées* sometimes had unexpected results. Winnaretta's efforts on behalf of Isadora Duncan not only launched the beautiful young American dancer on her European career, but eventually propelled her into the arms of Winnaretta's brother, Paris Singer, with whom the dancer bore a son.

Taking this in stride, Winnaretta continued to expand her patronage. Serge Diaghilev's arrival in Paris prompted her support of his ballets, danced by the likes of Nijinsky and Pavlova, and thrust her into the orbit of Stravinsky, whose powerfully raw music for *The Rite of Spring* nearly caused a riot in the newly opened Théâtre des Champs-Elysées in 1913. Eventually Winnaretta's connections led to a close friendship with Stravinsky and the establishment of Diaghilev's troupe as the revered Ballets Russes.

The 1920s brought her into contact with yet another avant-garde wave, this time led by Erik Satie and the Group of Six—including composers Milhaud, Poulenc, and Honegger—who frequented the famed café Le Boeuf sur le Toit (now at 34 Rue du Colisée, near the Champs-Elysées). In 1932 she commissioned Kurt Weill to write a symphony—his second, completed in 1934, as the winds of war began to rise.

Winnaretta herself fled to England during the German occupation of Paris, and died there in 1943. But this American princess lives on through her many commissioned works and through the Singer-Polignac Foundation, now headquartered in her beloved Avenue Georges-Mandel home, which continues her intelligent and adventurous tradition of giving.

Ox on the Roof

IT ALL BEGAN WITH AN IMPROBABLE LITTLE MAN IN A pince-nez and goatee who decisively upended the French musical scene during the grim years of the Great War. His name was Erik Satie, and in 1917 he emerged from obscurity with an astonishing score for an even more astonishing ballet, *Parade*. Incorporating parts for typewriters, sirens, and airplane propellers, *Parade* evoked everyday life—a mad mix of circus and the streets—and was like nothing that had ever been seen or heard before. Satie's collaborators in this fizzy venture included Pablo Picasso (costumes and sets) and Jean Cocteau (scenario). Serge Diaghilev's Ballets Russes performed Léonide Massine's choreography, and even the poet Guillaume Apollinaire contributed, writing the program notes.

Tout Paris was deliciously scandalized by this unquestionably avant-garde production, and soon after, Satie took the opportunity to launch several young composers who shared his vision.

He called them Les Nouveaux Jeunes, but by 1920 they had successfully tested Paris' artistic waters and become known as the Groupe des Six.

These six composers—Francis Poulenc, Darius Milhaud, Arthur Honegger, Georges Auric, Germaine Tailleferre, and Louis Durey, along with their spokesman, Jean Cocteau—delighted in each others' company. They took equal delight in setting the conventional world on its ear. In his entertaining memoirs, Milhaud tells how the group met every Saturday evening for two years at his home at 5 Rue Gaillard (now Rue Paul-Escudier, 9th) to have cocktails before moving on to a nearby restaurant on Rue Blanche. At both locations, they and their friends—who included musicians, poets, and painters—let loose. No serious discussions of art or theory for them! Yes, there was music, but there also were bicycle races around the dining-room table. In the spirit of things, unlikely ingredients surreptitiously made their way into the cocktail shaker.

After dinner, music, and more high jinks, the friends typically headed for the Fair of Montmartre or the circus, where they reveled in the crowds, the games of chance, and the blaring music. After that, they would return to Milhaud's, where they cheerfully sang, played, and read poetry.

Clearly not a pompous bunch, Les Six were completely at home in the music-halls of Maurice Chevalier and Mistinguett. They also adored the new American imports, ragtime and jazz. All of these popular influences found their way into Les Six's music, which—like Satie's—combined high art with low, and brought the rhythms and joy of the circus and the streets to even their most serious compositions.

One of the most famed of these was Milhaud's *Le Boeuf sur le Toit* (*The Ox on the Roof*), a musical fantasy based on the popular songs and rhythms of Brazil. (Having spent the war years there, Milhaud was familiar with its music and took the title from a Brazilian popular song.) Cocteau, ever on the alert for the new and the outrageous, used Milhaud's score as the basis for a surrealistic pantomime-ballet, whose climax called for a bartender to decapitate a policeman with a large fan, followed by a red-headed woman dancing—à la Salome—with the policeman's head. The production fostered a certain amount of hilarity and puzzlement, but significantly bolstered the group's notoriety.

Les Six published a slim volume of piano compositions and put on a ballet—*Les Mariés de la Tour Eiffel*—in which all manner of absurd disasters befall a wedding party at the Eiffel Tower. They also continued to present their compositions on an individual basis at several small halls around town. These included the Salle Huyghens, the cramped Montparnasse studio at 6 Rue Huyghens (14th) where Satie first took the group under his wing.

But now they were the Groupe des Six, and they were famous. After two years, their Saturday evenings were drawing an ever-larger and more fabulous crowd. Clearly, these artists required a more spacious venue, and Milhaud was eager to move the growing party out of his living room. The stories vary, but in all of them the composer and pianist Jean Wiener played a pivotal role, suggesting a small bar at 17 Rue Duphot (1st), near the Madeleine, called the Gaya. Milhaud was ecstatic, and the very next Saturday everyone headed for the Gaya. Both the music and the crowd were eclectic. Wiener played everything from jazz to Bach, and the throng included Diaghilev, Picasso, Maurice Chevalier, Satie, Cocteau, Anna de Noailles, Ravel, and Arthur Rubinstein.

With this illustrious crowd gracing his hangout, the Gaya's owner decided to move to a larger and more attractive location, at nearby 28 Rue Boissy d'Anglas (8th). Looking for just the right name, he hit upon Milhaud's ballet, *Le Boeuf sur le Toit*. And so the legendary Le Boeuf sur le Toit (the bar) began. Of course everyone came, and before long the name became shorthand for a particularly glittering and scintillating era. Anyone who was anyone in 1920s Paris made it a point to show up at Le Boeuf, to see and be seen.

Eventually Le Boeuf moved to 26 Rue de Penthièvre (8th) and 41 bis Avenue Pierre-1er-de-Serbie (8th) before settling

34 Rue du Colisée

into its present location at 34 Rue du Colisée (8th), just off the Champs-Elysées. By this time, Le Boeuf had become so popular and fashionable that the whole point of the original Saturday night revels had gradually disappeared. Sensing this, the old crowd drifted apart and moved on.

Satie had already broken with all of his former protégés save Milhaud, and—except for major anniversaries—the Groupe des Six no longer functioned as a group. This of course gave rise to speculation that there never had been much except friendship to link them together in the first place—a conclusion with which the group members themselves strongly agreed. Rugged individuals, with a decidedly individualistic approach to composition, they contended that they had simply shared a delightful moment of rebellion against Wagnerian and Impressionist music before each went his or her own way.

Still, whatever cold water Les Six have since dumped on the notion that they formed some sort of "school," their shared moment of rebellion remains an important one. Les Six made a lasting contribution to the course of contemporary music—sometimes in unexpected ways. In one particularly delightful reversal, the young future jazz great Dave Brubeck studied composition and jazz from Milhaud.

After several decades of neglect, works by Les Six—especially Poulenc, Honegger, and Milhaud—have once again been appearing on disks and concert programs. Yet for those who love Paris, the Groupe des Six will always be linked with a special time and place—1920s Paris and the ever-evocative Le Boeuf sur le Toit.

36.

An American in Paris

TAXI HORNS. SPECIFICALLY, PARIS TAXI HORNS. THEY must have made a big impression on George Gershwin, for when he returned to Paris in the spring of 1928, one of the first things he did was go hunting for them.

He had envisioned a major role for these honkers in *An American in Paris*, the new symphonic work he was writing. The first bars had appeared almost two years before, and he had already sketched out some of his major themes. But he needed something more, and at the first opportunity, he headed back to Paris for inspiration.

Soon after his arrival, he and a friend started out on foot from his suite in the Hôtel Majestic (then located on Avenue Kléber, 16th) to the Place de l'Etoile. After negotiating traffic around the Arc de Triomphe (no doubt dodging numerous taxis), they sauntered down the Avenue de la Grande-Armée (16th and 17th), which then sported a number of automobile shops. Gershwin was persistent, visiting every shop. He wanted exactly the right taxi horns—ones that sounded precisely the right notes. Gathering up his prizes, he brought them back to his hotel suite, where he piled them on top of the Steinway grand he had asked to be placed in the middle of the room.

There they were one day soon after, when a couple of young pianists (Mario Braggiotti and Jacques Fray) boldly knocked on Gershwin's door. They wanted to meet the famous American composer, and Gershwin—still in his dressing gown—was both amused and gracious. Inviting them in, he quickly noticed the two staring at his unusual collection. No, he explained, this wasn't some new American fad. He simply wanted to capture the traffic sounds of the Place de la Concorde during rush hour for the opening section of his new orchestral tone-poem, *An American in Paris*.

They were flattered when Gershwin asked them to help him out, to see if his bizarre idea worked. Explaining that the one gizmo played in A flat and the other in F sharp, he assigned a horn to each and asked them to join him in an impromptu concert. He would play the opening bars, and when he nodded his head, they were to squawk away in rhythm.

They did, and it worked. Thrilled to have played a role in

George Gershwin

the creation of such an obviously important piece of music, they departed on cloud nine. Gershwin, who in turn was duly impressed with the brief piano concert they had given him, kept up the friendship, providing their joint careers with an important boost when they came to the States.

A nice guy—as his many friends agreed. Also a very intense guy, who managed to cram more into a twenty-four-hour day than most people would ever care to consider. This Paris trip was billed as a working vacation, a time out from the constant demands of Gershwin's many musical comedy hits in New York and London so that he could rest, study, and compose. How much rest he got is certainly subject to question, but then again, Gershwin seemed to enjoy crowding his life with a million friends and activities.

In Paris, where he and his brother and collaborator, Ira, arrived at the Gare Saint-Lazare with their sister Frances, the social whirl immediately began. A crush of visitors constantly surrounded him, competing for his attention and feting him all over town. One of the most glamorous of these events was a bash that Elsa Maxwell gave for him in the garden of Laurent (still an elegant presence at 41 Avenue Gabriel, 8th) following the European premiere of his Concerto in F. Surrounded by Maxwell's coterie of displaced dukes and peripatetic royalty, the boy from Brooklyn was as relaxed and engaging as ever. Good-naturedly agreeing to play for the assembled guests (indeed, it was difficult to keep Gershwin away from the piano), he had a high old time and didn't get in until the wee hours of the morning.

Hobnobbing with the celebrities of 1920s Paris, Gershwin encountered an eclectic crowd, including Stravinsky, Prokofiev, Diaghilev, Maurice Chevalier, and Cole Porter. His encounter with Porter proved particular memorable. One evening the two played late into the night together, while Frances (Frankie) Gershwin sang. Porter (who then was living in style at 13 Rue Monsieur, 7th) was sufficiently impressed with Frankie's voice that he wrote her into his latest revue, where she did a brief star turn.

Despite constant late nights and nonstop daytime social engagements, Gershwin found time to play the tourist. He sauntered around Montmartre (where he encountered a girl, much as would his American in Paris). He also turned up at the Left Bank Mecca of Shakespeare and Company (then at 12 Rue de l'Odéon, 6th), where he charmed owner and publisher Sylvia Beach by buying a copy of *Ulysses*.

In spite of all the wonderful food, Gershwin sometimes yearned for hometown delicacies. In particular, he missed lox (smoked salmon) and went looking for some—after his bad French had disappointingly landed him with a lobster. He also paid his first visit to the Eiffel Tower, joining brother Ira in the adventure. Ira, always the more cautious and conservative of the two, found the height daunting, but both thoroughly enjoyed the view and even walked a good portion of the way down.

Somehow, in the midst of his packed schedule, George managed to put in serious composing time. Indeed, he seemed to work best when surrounded by noise—much as he did at his parents' Upper West Side residence, where until just the year before he had maintained bachelor quarters, composing in the midst of ongoing poker games and other hoopla.

His two months in Paris (which included event-packed side trips to Vienna and Berlin) certainly were productive, and he even found occasion to seek out Nadia Boulanger, to request lessons. Boulanger told him that he should stick to being Gershwin—an answer that Maurice Ravel had also given when Gershwin approached him earlier. Undeterred, Gershwin made the same request of Stravinsky, who asked Gershwin how much he made a year, then acerbically suggested that they reverse roles.

Whether Gershwin actually was seeking instruction or reassurance, it was abundantly clear that this once-unpromising son of Russian immigrant parents had already achieved remarkable success in both the popular and classical music worlds. George Gershwin (originally Gershovitz), a high-school dropout who had not encountered a piano until he was twelve, had rousingly conquered Tin Pan Alley and Broadway, then boldly ventured into the world of concert music.

The times were right for such a move. Darius Milhaud and the Groupe des Six had already introduced jazz into their compositions. Gershwin simply started from the other end, tenaciously acquiring the tools to express himself in the medium of Bach and Debussy, whose music he adored.

Rhapsody in Blue came first, followed by his Concerto in F. And now, *An American in Paris*. Somehow, even with everything else going on, Gershwin managed to complete about half of *An American in Paris* while he was in Paris, agreeing to let Walter Damrosch and the New York Philharmonic give the first performance. In December of that same year, Damrosch and the New York Philharmonic premiered *An American in Paris* at Carnegie Hall.

It was an immediate hit and has become a staple of the concert hall. The Gene Kelly movie only increased its audience and the enchantment. Here, in music, is the Paris that Gershwin loved, as seen by a strolling American visitor.

No doubt this visitor was Gershwin himself, for although countless Americans have since made this same journey of discovery, unquestionably Gershwin was his own American in Paris.

XIV

TIME OUT

37.

Lilac Café

LEGENDS ABOUND ON THE SUBJECT OF THE CLOSERIE des Lilas (171 Boulevard du Montparnasse, 6th), but one of the best concerns the painter Fernand Léger. He was sitting on the terrace of the Closerie one day, enjoying drinks and camaraderie, when he noticed a beautiful young bride riding a bicycle, her veil streaming in the wind.

Even for Montparnasse, where the unusual was common-place, this had all the earmarks of adventure. Jumping to his feet, Léger hailed the young woman, who came to a breathless stop. It was her wedding day—she was about to marry a notary's son—but one of the wedding gifts had been this bicycle. How could she resist a short ride? In any case, she hadn't been gone long—or, had she?

Rapidly consulting the clock, it turned out that she had sadly underestimated the length of her ride. But Léger, a handsome and gentle man, soon persuaded her that all was not lost. And indeed it wasn't, for not long after, the beautiful bicyclist became *his* wife.

Stories like this have put the Closerie on the map for more than a century. Frequented by Baudelaire, Strindberg, and

Oscar Wilde in the nineteenth century, when it was still a modest outdoor tavern, the Closerie acquired a new look and importance by the century's turn. By this time, Montparnasse was replacing Montmartre as center of Paris' art world, and the Closerie was becoming one of the hottest spots in Montparnasse. Writers and artists, including Picasso, Apollinaire, and Modigliani, gathered on its tree-shaded terrace to sip absinthe and argue endlessly over the topic of the moment.

But things change, and by the 1920s, when Ernest Hemingway discovered it, most of the Closerie's celebrities had drifted off to other Montparnasse cafés. Pleased by the quiet, Hemingway found himself a secluded table on the terrace and wrote *The Sun Also Rises*. He also read a manuscript by a young man named F. Scott Fitzgerald. Something called *The Great Gatsby*.

Hemingway, who gave the Closerie some priceless publicity in *A Moveable Feast*, is almost single-handedly responsible for its continued fame. Recognizing this, current management has given him star billing, with an upstairs banquet room called the Salon Ernest Hemingway. Downstairs, in the elegantly dark and mirrored bar, small nameplates recall other luminaries who have passed the time here, including Sartre, Beckett, Gide, and Simone de Beauvoir. Even Lenin seems to have been enough of a regular in the old days to earn a plaque. But Hemingway's stands alone, on the bar itself—a fitting location, by all accounts.

The Closerie's turn-of-the-century decor continues from bar to brasserie, where you can enjoy oysters or steak tartare, the house specialty. Restaurant and terrace are more garden-like, with the terrace actually under the trees. After decades of somnolence, the Closerie is now a romantic meeting place for the well-heeled and trendy, a much-prized clubhouse for celebrities and glitterati, who come to see and be seen.

Such ambiance can be pricey. But if you want a more affordable way to sample the undeniable Closerie charm, then stop by for drinks in the bar or terrace. Or eat in the brasserie, where a half-dozen Belon oysters plus steak tartare with frites will not unduly threaten your bank balance.

Oh—and what about the lilacs? It turns out that the Closerie never did have any. They belonged to a rival establishment, and the Closerie—mindful of the appeal—simply adopted the name.

Ice Cream Heaven

I COME FROM A FAMILY OF SERIOUS ICE CREAM LOVERS, and I married into an equally dedicated bunch—my father-in-law even got a Ph.D. in the stuff. So when I spotted a write-up on the window of Pascal Le Glacier proclaiming that no less an authority than Gault Millau had declared this the best ice cream in Paris, I took notice.

Not that there's anything wrong with Berthillon. The memory of Berthillon's melon sorbet draws me back into those infamous long lines every time I'm even remotely near the Ile Saint-Louis (31 Rue Saint-Louis-en-l'Ile). And if the melon is—gasp—*fini*, I'll happily sit up and beg for whatever flavor is left.

But Pascal Le Glacier, a relative newcomer, does indeed command a special place in the pantheon of Paris ice cream. Here in a charming corner of Passy (17 Rue Bois-le-Vent, 16th), Pascal Combette and his wife have established a sparkling shop specializing in some of the finest ice cream and sorbets you could ever hope to meet.

Their secret lies in perfection-driven hard work, superb ingredients, and long family tradition—including some splendid old family recipes. Pascal and his wife, who has four generations of *pâtissiers* and *chocolatiers* in her background, originally sold pastries and chocolates, but then decided that something was missing. In 1992 they branched into ice cream, and the rest is history.

Their product is proudly artisanal, or hand-crafted, and together they hand-make each small batch of sorbet and ice cream in a stunning array of sixty-eight flavors. Pascal Combette often puts in seventeen- to eighteen-hour days, especially for events such as weddings and birthdays. Madame Combette puts in almost as many hours, chopping fruit and nuts, making fresh fruit syrups for the sorbets, and preparing every mix before cream or water is added (only Evian is used). Somehow she finds time to raise a daughter and run the shop as well, taking time with each customer—whether consulting with Madame to coordinate dessert with dinner, or scooping a chocolate ice cream cone for a delighted youngster on his way home from school.

And the results? Oh, my. Sorbets? Try their rhubarb or mirabelle plum. Or their white peach or blood orange. You really can't go wrong—the flavors, fresh and true, positively sparkle. And the ice cream? Be daring and try the *réglisse* (licorice) or the *pain d'épices* (gingerbread). Then again, stick to simple (simple?) vanilla or chocolate for a bit of true perfection.

You can never go wrong with Pascal's Tahitian vanilla, while his chocolate ice cream is deeply chocolate, delectable whether you take it plain or mixed with cinnamon, orange peel, or a combination of dried fruit and nuts.

This is the sort of place that I wish would move in just around the corner from me. I would sample a new flavor every day and, in my fairy-tale world, would add not an ounce of weight. Just like Madame Combette herself, who mysteriously manages to maintain her youth and figure, even as she manages to maintain an atmosphere of serenity as she presides in her white lab coat over this pristine and inviting little corner of heaven.

NOTE: Pascal Le Glacier is closed Sundays and Mondays. Note that Pascal changes the flavor selection seasonally and does not carry fresh fruit sorbets or some ice cream flavors in winter.

39.

Flower Bowers

WHEN THAT CLASSIC BROADWAY MUSICAL, *Wonderful Town,* described a particularly delightful corner of New York as "a bit of Paree in Greenwich Village," it didn't have Baron Haussmann's boulevards in mind. Instead, it was summoning up images of all those appealing little cul-de-sacs tucked into unexpected corners of the glamorous City of Light.

Despite Haussmann's thorough remodeling of Paris, many of these picturesque places still remain. In fact, it's quite possible to fill any number of pleasant days tracking down such charming and unique destinations, shaping your search in any way you please. In my case, I decided to look for flowers. Or, more to the point, small enclaves whose very existence spoke of flowers. Cité Fleurie, Cité des Fleurs, and Cité Florale—all glorious-sounding destinations in springtime, or on a warm summer day.

The first on my list was the oldest of the three, the Cité des Fleurs. Located in the 17th arrondissement, not far from lovely

Parc Monceau, this long narrow lane runs between Avenue de Clichy and Rue de La Jonquière. You may enter at either end, although its Avenue de Clichy entrance is the easiest to get to, via the Brochant Métro stop. (Note that the street's gates close for the night at 7:30 P.M.)

This tranquil retreat dates from the mid-nineteenth century and was a planned community, with careful restrictions. Although the houses were not identical, they had to be compatible in style and size. Each had to have a front garden with flowering trees, while the fences and gates marched along (and still march) in similar size and style. Even the cast-iron vases that top the gateposts are exactly alike and, at least during the early years, displayed only approved kinds of flowers.

Well, that may sound a trifle rigid, but over the course of a century and a half, this flowery bower has softened its edges, maturing nicely. These attractive old dwellings display a variety of soft pastel colors as well as individualistic architectural details, including unexpected carvings and medallions, ornate windows, and some interesting entryways, including a sprinkling of curved double stairways.

Best of all, the trees and gardens have also matured well, providing the kind of oasis that the community's original planners had in mind. When I was there, only a camera crew shared the quiet and beauty of the morning with me, and we all kept our voices low. It seemed appropriate.

Shady, leafy, and bucolic, it's not surprising that many artists came to live and work here. Alfred Sisley, who had his studio at No. 27, is perhaps the best known of these. But

Cité Fleurie

despite appearances, this peaceful place did not always prove to be a refuge. A plaque at No. 25 tells passersby that during the German Occupation, members of the Resistance holed up here, forging papers. Unfortunately the Gestapo caught up with them, executing one (a woman) and sending the rest to their deaths in concentration camps.

An unsettling thought on such a beautiful morning, although not entirely an unexpected one. Charming havens like this quite naturally attracted artists and writers, many of whom held strong political convictions. The Resistance thrived in such out-of-the way places and, as it turned out, the Cité des Fleurs would not be the only flower bower with a Resistance story to tell.

Crossing to the Left Bank, I next visited the Cité Fleurie, located at 65 Boulevard Arago (13th). This beguiling bower grew up over a century ago in what was then a wasteland, on the city's outskirts. Much like its neighboring artist colony at La Ruche, in the 15th arrondissement, it was built from remnants of a World's Fair—in this case, the one of 1878. Hauling the materials here from the fair site, the builder constructed a series of rustic half-timbered artist studios in two long rows, divided by a long, woodsy garden.

The results, still enchanting today, soon drew a clientele of appreciative and impoverished artists, including many who would eventually become famous. Both Rodin and Maillol sculpted here, while Modigliani stayed at No. 9 and Gauguin (always impoverished) camped out with a friend.

Anti-Fascism as well as artists thrived in these sheltered studios. As early as the mid-1930s, an anti-Nazi library flourished at No. 18, where one could read literature unobtainable in Germany. During the Occupation, the Gestapo got wind of this subversive cache and shut it down, but only after it had been operating for several years.

After the war, Cité Fleurie continued its bucolic existence, but its low two-story buildings seemed a waste of space to some insensitive souls, who almost succeeded in demolishing it. Fortunately, its occupants, led by artist Henri Cadiou, tenaciously fought to protect it. At last, in 1973, they succeeded in making Cité Fleurie a protected site—a boon for the entire arrondissement as well as for those visitors fortunate enough to see it. Appropriately, the next-door park is named for the Cité's tireless protector, Henri Cadiou.

In contrast to both the Cité des Fleurs and Cité Fleurie, my third destination, the Cité Florale (also in the 13th arrondissement), is a jumble of tiny streets lined with equally tiny cottages of every imaginable style. This appealing pocket of Paris unexpectedly opens to the visitor from Rue Brillat-Savarin, just off Place de Rungis (an easy walk directly south from Cité Fleurie). My favorite entrance is via Rue des Liserons, which leads to the minute Square des Mimosas and picture-perfect Rue des Iris.

Yes, all the streets in this diminutive village are named after wildflowers and vines, including *liseron* (morning glory), *glycine* (wisteria), and orchids. All, with the exception of the unfortunate Rue des Orchidées, which has succumbed to a batch of apartment buildings, are an oasis miraculously preserved in the midst of uninspired high-rises.

One of the main reasons the Cité Florale still survives is that the ground beneath it will not support anything much taller and heavier. Built on a low-lying marshy area where the old Bièvre River spread into ponds, this small village grew up in the 1920s just inside the no-man's-land that bordered the Thiers fortifications. When these came down following World War I, development of the area soon followed. The Cité Florale was certainly the most inspired of this postwar building boom, and soon its winding streets and vine-covered cottages attracted a loyal group of residents, including writers and artists in search of low rents and charm.

Wander through this cluster of small streets and cul-de-sacs and soak up the beauty and the peace. No wonder flowers do well here, and one assumes that its residents—and their artistic endeavors—are also thriving.

XV

WALKING, RUNNING, SHOPPING

40.

Viaduc des Arts

FORGET THE LEFT BANK FOR THE MOMENT. A NEW HOT spot has emerged on the Right Bank, encompassing the narrow streets of the Marais through the cafés of the Place de la Bastille. This mecca for the young and hip now extends eastward to Avenue Daumesnil's sparkling new Viaduc des Arts (12th), home of a rejuvenated arts and crafts movement and some of the trendiest shopping in Paris.

Located beneath the arches of a former elevated railway linking the Place de la Bastille to Vincennes, the *ateliers* (workshops) of the recently refurbished viaduct have emerged as a showcase for an astonishing variety of craftsmen. All of these invite you to watch them at work—either over their shoulders or through huge windows fronting the street. Appropriately located in the Faubourg Saint-Antoine district, historic home of Paris crafts, each of the Viaduc's many arches houses specialists—from glassblowers, leather workers, tapestry-weavers, and silversmiths to repairers of antique fabrics, musical instruments, and dolls.

Learn how to embroider at Le Bonheur des Dames (17 Avenue Daumesnil), or purchase a prepared kit. Check out the stonecutter at Ripamonti (13 Avenue Daumesnil) and the porcelain painters at Atelier Le Tallec (93/95 Avenue Daumesnil), or any of a variety of furniture and cabinet makers along the way. If retouching photographs is not your interest, then perhaps the hatmaker will appeal. You have a world of creativity at your fingertips here, to purchase and to enjoy.

One of my favorites, the Atelier N'O (21 Avenue Daumesnil), specializes in a variety of already-created and do-it-yourself decorative items conjured out of natural and recycled materials. "We want to work with the five senses," says Thierry Durot, Atelier N'O's director. "Music for the ear, beauty for the eye, incense to smell—and so many things to touch." He pauses thoughtfully. "And of course," he adds, "you will talk with us."

Of course. Because creativity, and the joy of encouraging the creative process, is what Atelier N'O is all about. Founded by Marc and Evelyne Viladrich, N'O (from "Nomades Authentic") has been located for several years here in the Viaduc des Arts. During that time it has grown from a workshop dedicated to providing natural, recyclable, and recycled objects into one of the most chic shopping experiences in Paris.

Simply walk by, and the windows beckon. Once inside, the sense of discovery grows. Wheeled pushcarts, themselves recycled objects, stylishly display baskets and trays of dried pods, cones, peppers, cinnamon sticks, shells, starfish, coconut shells, and gourds. Bottles filled with different textures and colors of sand line the walls, while buckets loaded with exotic-looking pebbles and stones artistically crowd the floor.

This is the section, called "Trésors de nature," where you can create your own little Zen garden in the gourd bowl of your choice. Staff members are on hand to help you make your selection, but they are just as happy to let you wander aimlessly, picking your own treasures for whatever purpose you have in mind.

Care for an exotic tree root? N'O has a wonderful selection, stuck in corners here and there. What about an ancient-looking Amazon canoe? N'O has a beauty. Enhance your home naturally, with hanging lanterns, imported fabrics, natural home fragrances (coffeewood, balsam, and lotus) or a lamp made of shells. Organize your life with file folders and boxes of recycled cardboard. Luxuriate in rose water, or scrub up with attractive soaps in steel gray and bronze.

The variety is almost endless, and there are two floors to explore—accompanied by the soft beat of World Music. A dramatic split staircase leads up to a small cabin, a kind of treehouse in the jungle. This in turn displays a variety of exotic goods, including masks. Fall in love with something already made, or make it yourself—N'O offers an enormous array of possibilities.

It is this sense of possibility and discovery that is so marked here. Sophisticated customers with the delighted expressions of small children approach the cash register bearing their discoveries—a bottle of rose-colored marbles or a carefully selected array of shells. They will undoubtedly return.

I came on a specific quest, looking for flat stones for a homemade fountain—one that would incorporate some of the interesting rocks and pebbles we have collected on our travels. My salesperson contemplated this request. Flat stones? No, he did not think they had any. But perhaps there was something in storage.

Plunging down to the cellar, he rummaged for several minutes before triumphantly returning with three small, flat, and extremely dusty paving stones. Bearing the faint imprint of some distant Asian city, they were perfect. With great seriousness, he carefully wrapped each in pink tissue paper and sent me on my way.

Yes, I will return to this extraordinary workshop, and to its equally extraordinary neighbors. Often.

NOTE: The Viaduc des Arts is located on Avenue Daumesnil, 12th, just beyond the Opéra Bastille. Some of the items carried at N'O cannot be brought into the United States.

41.

Promenade Plantée

AFTER EXPLORING THE SHOPS AND *ateliers* OF THE
Viaduc des Arts (Avenue Daumesnil, 12th), you may be ready
for a break. Yes, you can stop for coffee or lunch at the Viaduc
Café. Or you can rest and relax in the Promenade Plantée.

This inviting elevated garden isn't difficult to find. Look for
a stairway—any of several—between the Viaduc's shops. Follow
the steps upward and you'll find yourself in another world—an
extended promenade that gracefully inhabits the right-of-way
of the elevated railroad that once chugged back and forth here,
between the Place de la Bastille and Vincennes.

Once here, you can rest beneath the arbors and even take a
snooze. But if you're inclined to walk, you have a treat ahead.
For this narrow urban oasis stretches imaginatively through a
part of Paris you may not know, from the Viaduc's first atelier,
at the corner of Avenue Daumesnil and Rue de Lyon, right to
the eastern edge of Paris.

Here, along the rooftops of the Viaduc des Arts, you will find an *allée* surrounded by arbors and trellises, comfortable benches and trees. Well-designed and maintained, the Promenade Plantée rewards the stroller with unfolding variety, including an abundance of roses in season and two lavender-edged pools. Sit and relax a bit or saunter along, taking the opportunity to look out over this freshly rejuvenated part of the city.

The Viaduc des Arts ends at Rue de Rambouillet, but the Promenade pleasantly continues, providing new surprises along the way—including a couple of architecturally interesting "walk-throughs" between apartment buildings. At Rue Montgallet, the Promenade crosses a long pedestrian arch over the Jardin de Reuilly, a many-layered park on the site of the railway's vanished switching yards. More romantically, this site once sheltered the Château de Reuilly, home to the Merovingian kings.

Just beyond this urban oasis, the Promenade turns into the street-level Allée Vivaldi, an attractive boulevard along the former railroad right-of-way. The handsome old Reuilly train station is still standing at the Allée Vivaldi's far end, where a bike path joins the Promenade. Soon after, the Promenade dives into a series of tunnels—refreshed by waterfalls, pools, and hanging vines. Eventually it reemerges into a garden passageway below street level.

There are any number of small delights along the way, such as the maze near the Rue de Reuilly, where you can cheat a bit by climbing a small stairway leading to an observation point. And, of course, there is an abundance of greenery everywhere.

You can branch to the right at Square Charles-Péguy, an attractive park commemorating a young poet from the neighborhood who died in World War I. Or you can continue on a bit to the Périphérique, where a spiral staircase takes you to a small frontage road and another bike path. From there, you are within a breath of the Bois de Vincennes.

This leisurely three-mile walk is just the thing for a break. Or for whenever you would like to stretch a bit and discover a newly vibrant part of Paris.

42.

Pen Ultimate

"Everything begins with writing," proclaims my newly acquired pen catalogue. How could one doubt it, after a visit to that temple of penmanship, Elysées Stylos Marbeuf?

The French have fortunately placed fine pens and writing supplies in their pantheon of the necessities of life, along with the best in fashion, dining, and perfume. Paris is dotted with fine stationers, and the Galeries Lafayette carry a particularly impressive array of pens. But for a truly memorable introduction to this grand French tradition, pay a visit to Elysées Stylos Marbeuf.

Located at 40 Rue Marbeuf (8th), just around the corner from the Champs-Elysées, this prestigious yet approachable little shop—in business since 1949—radiates a calm professionalism. Busy even on weekday mornings, its six salespeople rim the counters, ready to help. After all, they love pens, too, and their job is to match you up with just the right one.

This involves many considerations, including appearance and price. Most important is the way the pen feels in the hand. Length, shape, balance, and the correct nib (or point) are essential, and Stylos Marbeuf's salespersons are well aware that a pen—even an extremely expensive one—must feel exactly right, or you will not enjoy using it. Selecting from an impressive array of prestigious brands, they patiently assist a wide range of customers, from complete novices to collectors.

My husband, who loves the feel of writing with a well-made fountain pen, already knew what he wanted: something with heft, a solid-gold nib, and preferably a Waterman. He gazed for several minutes at the shop window before entering, joined by a steady stream of interested passers-by, all of whom were obviously taken with the display. But having thoroughly enjoyed his previous Waterman, my husband was intent on acquiring another—and in Paris, which seemed appropriate, since Waterman has been most thoroughly French for almost a half century.

Originally it was American. Back in 1884 Lewis E. Waterman invented the modern fountain pen, doing away with dip pens and primitive reservoir types, which were inclined to blotch. Other inventive Americans, including George Parker and Walter Sheaffer, soon followed. Despite patent wars, litigation and the Great Depression, these giants thrived until mid-century, when ballpoint pens began to make serious inroads. The French Baron Bich and his disposable Bic pens soon won this war, leaving Waterman, Parker, and Sheaffer with the smaller upscale market. In 1954, Waterman shut down its United States manufacturing facilities, leaving its French subsidiary to carry on—its logo becoming "Waterman Paris." Parker eventually moved to England.

The knowledgeable saleswoman pleasantly guided my husband to exactly the right pen, fitted it up with the correct nib, and then wrapped it beautifully for him. Adding to our delight, she then gift-wrapped the little box of extra ink cartridges. Completely enchanted, we reluctantly left.

Of course we will visit here again. But next time it will be my turn.

43.

Village Saint-Paul

SUNDAY AFTERNOONS AND THE VILLAGE SAINT-PAUL were made for each other. I love wandering through this maze of picturesque courtyards, poking around in the antique shops, and stopping to chat with an artist friend whose studio overlooks the ancient ruins of Paris' twelfth-century walls.

Who knows what you may find? Perhaps a pair of 1920s Quimper plates or a piece of eighteenth-century china. Or perhaps a Pauline doll (circa 1830–40) and a tiny trunk full of antique doll clothing. Then again, you may be attracted by prints, vintage photos, and music. Or antique chandeliers, furniture and clocks. Brides with a taste for old silver and china can register at Histoires de Table, specializing in table decor from 1800 to 1950.

The Village Saint-Paul, encompassing the pedestrian enclave between Rue Saint-Paul, Rue de l'Ave Maria, Rue Charlemagne, and Rue des Jardins-Saint-Paul (4th), and

Village Saint-Paul

spreading along some of the streets alongside, is filled with small shops specializing in a wide variety of high-quality art and antiques. My most recent find was an eye-catching pair of neo-Renaissance French doors, bearing cameos of a helmeted knight and his lady. Not having the 960 Euros—or the space—for such an acquisition, I left them for someone else, but I enjoyed "owning" them for a few minutes in the old passage-way where the owner had propped them.

The Village is a hidden jewel of the Marais, that picturesque quarter on the Right Bank that has found new life after a couple of dismal centuries. Until recently, even Parisians barely remembered that Charles V once lived here, having moved from the Cité to the vicinity of the Bastille after his encounter with Etienne Marcel and an angry mob. Charles lived for a time at the Hôtel Saint-Pol, or Saint-Paul, and the French nobility soon followed. During the next couple of centuries, the entire quarter enjoyed a sumptuous building boom, capped by Henri IV's splendid Place Royale (now Place des Vosges).

Only when Louis XIV moved the royal court to Versailles did the Marais fall out of fashion, dipping into a shabby neglect that worsened over the years. But after some bad centuries, the quarter has once again come into its own—an historic preservation district that throbs with nightlife, good food, and great shopping. The Village Saint-Paul—a pleasing network of old buildings and courtyards on what once were the gardens of Charles V's Hôtel Saint-Pol—is one of the Marais' most unexpected discoveries.

Come here to browse and shop, even on Sundays. Come to watch artists and restorers hard at work, or simply strike up a conversation with one of the shopkeepers. It's not difficult to do, especially if you share a particular passion.

And if you want to see the Village in quite a different light, return at night—by moonlight, if possible. Wander from courtyard to courtyard. Climb the terraced steps and drift through old archways, shadowed in the lamplight. Sit in the tiny park beneath a tree and look out over the shops, whose displays are now safely behind locked doors. Tomorrow morning, these displays will be arrayed across the cobblestones, and the crowds will mingle pleasantly. But for now, in the moonlight, the Village Saint-Paul is all your own.

NOTE: Most shops in the Village Saint-Paul are open afternoons, Thursday–Monday.

44.

Marathon

AT THE SIGNAL, THE FIRST OF AN ELITE GROUP OF runners crossed the starting line, trotting down the Champs-Elysées from the Arc de Triomphe toward the Place de la Concorde. In a breathtaking instant, almost thirty thousand runners surged after them, packing every inch of the avenue as far as the eye could see.

It was the opening of the 2001 Paris Marathon. Athletes had been pouring into the city for days, collecting their bibs (the identifying numbers worn over their running gear), visiting the marathon's Expo, and checking out the route—portions of which had flooded owing to unusually heavy rains in the days and weeks before.

Having hosted marathons for more than a century, Paris was ready. Marathon organizers provided not only the usual array of food, water, sponges, and medical services along the route, but had staged a show for the runners and their supporters. Thirty orchestras, ten brass bands, two Latin bands, and nine street-theater shows added a particularly Parisian sense of festivity to the 42.195 km ordeal.

Yes, that's 26.2 miles, and it's a long way for anyone to

walk, let alone run. Amazingly, of the nearly twenty-eight thousand runners and two dogs who started the race, more than twenty-two thousand completed the course within the five hours and forty minutes allowed. (Sorry—no word on the dogs' endurance or times.)

More than eleven hundred runners completed the distance in less than three hours, while the first- and second-place winners of the men's race (both Kenyans) battled to a photo finish in just over two hours (2.09.40). In a Kenyan sweep, the fastest woman came in at 2.27.53, while in an awe-inspiring feat of arms, the Handisport victor (a Frenchman) powered his wheelchair to a 1.37.44 victory.

None of these were record times—rain and cold prevented that. But it still was thrilling to run along a course that stretched through the heart of Paris to the Bois de Vincennes, then back again along the Seine to the Bois de Boulogne and the finish at Avenue Foch, near where it all began.

Among the many Americans who entered, Abbe Krieger, a New Yorker with three New York marathons under her belt, managed to take in some of the sights as she ran. It was incredible, she told me, to be jogging along in that crowd down the Champs-Elysées toward the Grande Roue (giant Ferris wheel) on the Place de la Concorde. And it was just as fantastic to be returning along the Seine route with the Eiffel Tower on her left.

The very first Paris marathon took place in 1896, not long after the modern Olympics began, and drew a grand total of 191 runners. Life was simpler then, with some of the participants running barefoot. The winner, an Englishman, seems to have worn shoes, but gratefully downed a glass of champagne as he neared the end of the course. This characteristic French touch has continued to the present, for Abbe reported that, much to her surprise, wine was served up at Mile 18. Perhaps the wine wasn't official, but whatever its source, she thought it provided a wonderfully French method of easing the pain.

The wine definitely made an impression, but the Paris touch that Abbe particularly appreciated was the Easter Bunny street performer who gave her candy eggs and marshmallow rabbits as she slogged through the rain in the Bois de Boulogne, near the end of the course. Having slipped to the back of the pack, thanks to a bout with flu only days before, she needed all the encouragement she could get. Somehow, the whimsical bunny gave her the boost she needed to get to the finish line.

And once across, what did she do? Having fantasized throughout the entire marathon about the chocolate croissant she had passed up at breakfast, Abbe's first post-race reward was obvious. Then, following a massage, leg-icing, and a bath, she went out on the town. Sleep? That could wait. After months of training and a punishing race, it was time to celebrate.

XVI

DOWN BELOW

45.

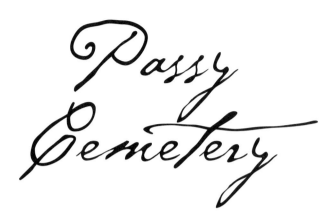

Passy Cemetery

"You are looking for Bao Dai?" The cheerful little man had popped up among the tombstones like some sort of French elf, smiling as he drew closer.

"Why, yes," I replied, wondering how he knew—and for that matter, wondering exactly where he had come from. The tombstones of Passy Cemetery are densely packed, and I had thought I was alone.

He smiled more broadly, pleased that his hunch was correct, and even more pleased that he could be of assistance. "Over here," he told me, leading the way down a narrow path toward a very flat and unornamented stone. Not a tombstone, to be sure, but merely a cover, without so much as an inscription.

I frowned, clearly puzzled, and he smiled again, delighted at my bafflement. "His wife is still living," he explained of the tomb's inhabitant, the last emperor of Vietnam. "He will get his tombstone after she dies."

"But how will she fit?" I asked, still a little confused. I had already seen the large family vaults of the many wealthy Parisians who are buried here, including the Renault family. This looked more like a single-occupancy arrangement. "The tomb is narrow."

He chuckled. "It is simple," he told me. "They stack them up, one on top of another, like so." And he demonstrated, one hand above the other.

"Oh, I see," I exclaimed, light dawning. "I've just been to the tomb of Berthe Morisot, who is buried with her husband Eugène Manet and brother-in-law Edouard Manet, along with Edouard's wife. It's a small tomb, and I couldn't figure out how it held them all."

He nodded. "Did you know that Berthe Morisot's daughter, Julie, is also buried here? Julie Manet?"

The beauteous Julie? The one so lovingly painted by Renoir as well as by her famous mother? No, I didn't, and soon he was off and running, showing me this sight and that. I had already picked up a map at the cemetery's administrative office and checked out the registries there, but my new friend—an amateur historian—was a wealth of information about this wonderful small cemetery in the heart of Paris.

Passy Cemetery (2 Rue du Commandant-Schloesing, 16th) is a magnet for those in the know who care about Paris' cultural past. Here in this peaceful tree-shaded oasis adjoining the Place du Trocadéro lie famous composers such as Claude Debussy, Gabriel Fauré, and Jacques Ibert; painters such as Edouard Manet and Berthe Morisot; writers such as Jean

Giraudoux; entertainers and stars such as the beloved Fernandel, plus a number of others, including *couturier* Jean Patou and aviation pioneers Henri Farman and Dieudonné Costes (France's Charles Lindbergh).

The most aristocratic of Paris cemeteries, Passy is the final resting place for captains of industry, statesmen (including the assassinated Georges Mandel), and financiers, as well as exiled royalty such as Emperor Bao Dai and the young Iranian princess who entered with such a splash only a few months before I visited (her tomb was still blanketed with rose petals and flowers).

The most fascinating aspect of this peaceful place is its collection of funerary sculpture—some of it (especially the nineteenth-century entries) astonishingly maudlin and some, executed by sculptors such as Rodin, Landowski, Dunikowski, and Zadkine, of extraordinary quality and power. You could easily spend an entire afternoon here simply totting up your own personal list of the best and the worst.

Grief-stricken females abound. An especially dramatic one lies prone on the grave of Henriette Lafourcade, in the cemetery's southwest corner, while an attractive nude modestly kneels on the tomb of the Famille Albert Laurans, along the central walkway. An overwrought angel stands guard over the Rodocanchi family, while a downright disturbing bas-relief of a nineteenth-century child, complete with hat, stares malevolently out from a tombstone near the Manet family grave.

Berthe Morisot and the Manet clan opted for simple elegance (as did Debussy, Ibert, and Fauré), but there are plenty of others who did not. The Perényi family has erected a full-sized Pietà above their last resting place, while the Famille de San Fernando has placed a life-sized sculpture of a biblically attired woman at their sepulcher door, bearing a garland of flowers. Top prize for astounding funerary art, though, has to go to the Famille Madrenas y Satorres, although the chapel created for painter Marie Bashkirtseff (complete with her last painting) comes close. In contrast with all this emotion, Jean Giraudoux occupies a tiny peaceful garden, covered with vines, while Dieudonné Costes has a biplane and relief maps of his transatlantic flights.

It certainly leads one to speculate about the personalities and styles of these permanent residents of Passy's elegant City of the Dead. And it offers a rare opportunity to check out the last accommodations of an especially interesting group of people.

Try it. You'll enjoy the peace and—who knows?—you may run into my informative friend.

NOTE: You'll find the Landowski bas-relief of Henri Farman in the southeast portion of the cemetery, within sight of the powerful—and towering—Dunikowski sculpture. Rodin's medallion of Jehan de Bouteiller is nearby. Paul Guillaume's tomb, with Zadkine's bas-relief, is located near the cemetery entrance.

46.

Down a Hidden Staircase

High on the slopes of Belleville, at the corner of Rue Augustin-Thierry and Rue Compans (19th) stands a mysterious small round building with a distinctive cupola. Windowless, and with its one solitary door bolted shut, it looks like a secret meeting place for some forgotten sect. But its true purpose turns out to be quite different from anything you might suppose. This small building is the Regard de la Lanterne, and it once presided over an ancient and important source of water—the medieval aqueduct of Belleville.

This is a story that takes one down hidden staircases and even unexpected manholes into the remains of a system that supplied Parisians with drinking water for hundreds of years. It reveals a side of Paris that today's visitors, or even natives, might not even suspect. Because oddly enough, for a city built along a major river, Paris and Parisians have spent the better part of two thousand years battling a chronic lack of water.

In part, this was a problem of finding sufficiently clean water. But to a large extent, it was a matter of finding water at all. Those who lived beyond or above the banks of the Seine faced an everyday challenge of water supply. This grew infinitely worse during the summer, when the river—then much wider and shallower than today— sank into marshes and mud, leaving many Parisians quite literally high and dry.

The Romans first recognized the problem and addressed it with their customary decisiveness. Having settled the slopes of the Left Bank rather than the boggy marshes along the river, they soon realized that if they were going to supply their thermal baths and homes with enough water, they were going to have to do something besides lug the stuff up the hill from the river. Not having the means to lift it from the Seine, they looked for another solution. Soon they discovered it to the south, in the Rungis area, where they found spring water that they could bring in by gravity, letting it flow gently into their city through a narrow covered channel. It was a major undertaking, approximately ten miles from source to destination, and required a dramatic aqueduct-bridge en route over the Bièvre river valley at what today is Arcueil. (Vestiges of this remarkable structure still remain in Arcueil, and you can admire fragments at the Musée Carnavalet, 23 Rue de Sévigné, 3rd.)

The Gallo-Romans seemed to take this sophisticated system

well in stride—at least until the surge of barbarian attacks in the late third century sent them flying to their fortified island in the Seine (now the Ile de la Cité). Without regular maintenance, their extraordinary aqueduct slowly deteriorated, until it all but disappeared.

Now Parisians had to fall back on Seine water, although by this time, a growing number were digging wells. This turned out to be a far easier task on the Right Bank than on the Left, where the water table lay much deeper beneath the surface. This water tasted good and seemed clean, but unfortunately was far from pristine. The very fact that it lay close to the surface meant that it received run-off from Paris' notoriously muddy streets, as well as seepage from its open sewers.

Of course, it wasn't until well into the nineteenth century that anyone drew a connection between the quality of the water they drank and the epidemics that regularly swept the city. Instead, for centuries they merely drank up, with the more finicky either filtering the liquid or simply allowing it to settle before quaffing.

Indeed, the main qualification for water was availability, and in the twelfth century, as Paris began to revive from its earlier encounters with the Vikings, its intrepid citizens once again began to hunt for water. Competition became especially fierce on the Right Bank, whose population was booming—probably in large part because of the relative ease with which Parisians could dig wells there. Increasingly, those on the Right Bank who lived a fair piece from the Seine found they couldn't rely on well water alone, and before long two wealthy Right Bank abbeys began to scout out the possibility of bringing in spring water by aqueduct from the north.

In those days, lots of little springs trickled down the bucolic hills of Belleville and Ménilmontant (street names like Rue des Cascades and Rue de la Mare, 20th, still summon up their memory). These *sources du Nord*, or springs of the North, looked especially promising, since they burbled out of the ground at a height that made it possible to bring their waters down by simple gravity to thirsty Parisians.

The monks of Saint-Lazare were probably the first to tap these waters. Their priory was located well outside the medieval city of Paris, along the route then known as the Chaussée de Saint-Lazare (now Rue du Faubourg-Saint-Denis), at present-day Boulevard de Magenta, 10th. Toward the end of the twelfth century, these monks began to harness the spring waters that spurted up near the village of Pré-Saint-Gervais, just over the present-day northeastern boundary of Paris, bringing these waters by conduit to their priory.

About the same time, or perhaps a little after, the monks of Saint-Martin-des-Champs harnessed the waters of Belleville, bringing them by conduit to their abbey—located along the old Roman road into Paris (now Rue Saint-Martin), at present-day Rue Réaumur, 3rd. (You can still see the shell of their extraordinary abbey church, which now houses the Musée des Arts et Métiers.)

The waters of Belleville at first flowed through several different aqueducts, including a joint effort between Saint-Martin-des-Champs and the Templars, whose land it crossed. Another

Regard de la Lanterne

small system brought water to the seventeenth-century Hôpital Saint-Louis (2 Place du Docteur-Alfred-Fournier, 10th). In time, as the City of Paris took over this water supply, most of these systems were linked, combining their flow.

But at first, these aqueducts were separate and surprisingly simple affairs, with the spring water collected in covered stone-lined trenches known as *pierrées*. These *pierrées*, which ran just above a bed of impermeable clay, ended at small basins or settling pools placed inside buildings called "regards."

That is where the Regard de la Lanterne comes in. Its job, as the head regard in its system, was to collect the water from its pierrées and send it, via aqueduct, along its way. It also served to protect the precious water it collected from pollution (primarily cattle) and thieves (mostly the two-legged variety).

Descend the hidden steps that sweep downward in a double staircase, just inside the regard's door. There, at the bottom, you will see three pipes leading in from the regard's *pierrées*, whose water flows into a small pool. From there, the water flows out via an ancient aqueduct, built during the fifteenth and sixteenth centuries, replacing the far simpler version that preceded it.

Bring a flashlight, because it's difficult to see in all this darkness. If you train your light along the wall, you can make out a name carved there in 1586, only three years after this regard was built. You can also stand at the entrance to the aqueduct, which is an elaborate stone tunnel more than six

Regard de la Lanterne, interior

feet high and three feet wide. Here the water flows from the basin along a shallow channel in the aqueduct's floor. What is surprising is how little there is.

From the Regard de la Lanterne, the water of Belleville once traveled along this ancient aqueduct, encountering other regards along the way. Originally there were about forty regards in the Belleville and Pré-Saint-Gervais systems, which either collected water from several sources or divided water to send it to its users. Other regards simply served as settling pools. Their functions varied, and few regards still remain—although all are now, most fortunately, protected as *Monuments Historiques*.

Several regards from the Pré-Saint-Gervais aqueduct still exist, including the Fountain of Pré-Saint-Gervais, located in the town's Place de la Mairie. In the Belleville aqueduct, the Regard de la Lanterne is by far the most dramatic, but three others, all nearby, are also interesting: the Regard Saint-Martin (42 Rue des Cascades); the Regard des Messiers (17 Rue des Cascades); and the Regard de la Roquette (behind 36-38 Rue de la Mare). The Regard Saint-Martin, whose waters originally supplied both the abbey of Saint-Martin-des-Champs and the Templars, is the handsomest of these. Messiers and Roquette, whose waters were part of another small system, are less imposing. In the eighteenth century, all three of these and their aqueducts were finally joined to the aqueduct of Belleville.

Oddly enough, there never was much water in either the Belleville or Pré-Saint-Gervais systems. To make matters worse, the water itself—although reasonably pure—was heavily flavored by the limestone and gypsum through which it ran, making it unpleasant to drink. Still, monarchs and the City of Paris all tried over the years to make as much of this water as possible available to the people of Paris. As early as the twelfth century, King Philip Augustus arranged with the monks of Saint-Lazare to take some of their water, via pipes (probably lead), down present-day Rue Faubourg Saint-Denis and Rue Saint-Denis to the Fontaine des Innocents (grandly rebuilt in the 1500s and later moved to what now is Place Joachim-du-Bellay, 1st). This water also supplied a fountain in the new covered markets, or Halles. Other fountains followed, and during the Middle Ages, water from Pré-Saint-Gervais ran in all the public fountains located on or to the west of Rue Saint-Denis, while fountains located to the east received their water from Belleville.

During the fourteenth and fifteenth centuries, the City of Paris—aided by the upheavals of the Hundred Years War—gradually took over the water and aqueducts of Belleville and Pré-Saint-Gervais. But these waters never supplied more than a fraction of what was needed, and in any case seemed better for washing than for drinking. By the mid-eighteenth century, the water of Belleville primarily cleaned the sewers, while the somewhat better-tasting water of Pré-Saint-Gervais supplied Paris until the 1860s, when it was routed into the sewers—where some still runs today.

Just as several of the historic regards still remain, so do portions of the aqueducts that once served them. A section of the narrow aqueduct leading to the Hôpital Saint-Louis has somehow survived the inroads of urbanization, while several pieces of the Belleville aqueduct still run beneath the houses and streets of Belleville. Its course is marked by ancient stone markers, to facilitate repairs as well as to protect it from damage—although much damage has already been done. Still, what remains is now protected as a *Monument Historique* and, with the active oversight of the deeply committed Association Sources du Nord–Etudes et Préservation (ASNEP), its survival seems more secure.

While denizens of the Right Bank were receiving waters from the sources du Nord, the Left Bank was feeling quite left out—that is, until the early seventeenth century, when an imperious queen decided to build the extraordinary Luxembourg Palace for herself, complete with extensive gardens and fountains. Since water was not available in the quantities she required, Marie de Medici sent engineers scurrying to look for new sources. Bits and pieces of the old Gallo-Roman aqueduct had already surfaced, attracting the attention of her late husband, Henri IV. His assassination interrupted plans to reconstruct the aqueduct, but now Marie took up the huge enterprise.

Work began in 1612 and continued for years, following the approximate course of the old Gallo-Roman watercourse. At last, in 1623, spring water from Rungis traveled the eight-mile underground channel, crossing the Bièvre at almost the same point where the Gallo-Romans had positioned their aqueduct-bridge all those centuries before, and arriving in Paris just south of the Luxembourg Gardens. En route, the water passed through twenty-seven regards, several of which still survive. A small one is perched on a hill behind the La Rochefoucauld nursing home, on Avenue René-Coty, 14th. The last and grandest, the Maison du Fontainier, rises behind a wall at 42 Avenue de l'Observatoire, 14th. This was where the waters from Rungis were divided between Marie de Medici's grand new Luxembourg Palace, several public fountains, and a number of religious communities. The waters of Rungis fed the Medici Fountain in the Luxembourg Gardens until 1904, and today flow into Parc Montsouris' peaceful lake.

Much like its sister aqueducts to the north, though, this aqueduct never lived up to expectations. In part, this was because of the number of concessions handed out. But even more important was the disappointing amount of water this aqueduct managed to deliver. Despite its aqueduct, the Left Bank still had to look to wells and the river for its water. And the Seine continued to play almost as important a role as before.

Over the following years, Paris employed an extraordinary number of devices to step up the water supply, including Henri IV's huge Samaritaine water pump on the Pont-Neuf (finally dismantled in 1813, after a long and hard-working career) and its sister Notre-Dame water pump on Pont Notre-Dame (which survived until 1858). Along the way, steam pumps and artesian wells had their day, as well as Napoléon's grand Canal de l'Ourcq, which served as a navigation system as well as water supply.

It was Baron Haussmann who, with his determined engineer, Eugène Belgrand, established the far-flung water system that, with modifications and updating, still supplies Paris today. Well before the role of water in spreading epidemics became widely known, Haussmann set to work to create a vast system of covered aqueducts and reservoirs to convey and store enormous quantities of pure spring water from afar. It was a daring move, but in a way no more so than the Gallo-Romans who engineered their aqueduct of Arcueil, or the medieval Parisians who built the little Regard de la Lanterne.

NOTE: To visit the Regard de la Lanterne, contact the Association Sources du Nord–Etudes et Préservation (Tel: 01-43-49-36-91; E-mail: asnep@free.fr).
To visit the Maison du Fontainier, contact Paris Historique (Tel: 01-48-87-74-31; E-mail: contact@paris-historique.org).
Both sites are open during Journées du Patrimoine, the third weekend of every September.

XVII

HANDS ACROSS the SEA

47.

Paris, 9/11

On hearing my American accent, the museum attendant placed her hand over her heart. "I love America," she said fervently. "And I *love* New York." An attendant at another museum refused to accept payment for admission. It was the least he could do, he told us earnestly—as a gesture of solidarity between the French and American people.

At a train station in the Paris suburbs, a young ticket seller seemed almost overcome by the fact that he was facing a couple of Americans—and New Yorkers at that. With great emotion, he fervently told us how deeply touched he was by the terrible events in our country.

Yes, there was the concierge at our hotel who wanted us to know that Paris had suffered proportionately as much over the years from terrorist attacks. And yes, a new acquaintance, although distraught over the attacks, felt that America had to some degree brought these terrible events upon itself by its complacency and insistence on going it alone.

But more typical was the owner of an upscale Paris ice cream shop, who spent almost an hour talking with us about the need for people around the world to connect with one another. "Let us forget about politics and politicians!" she exclaimed at one point. "We are all one family, and we must hold together."

When we finally had to leave, she would not let us pay for the ice cream we had eaten. "Give the money to a church," she told us with a warm smile, as she escorted us to the door. "Light a candle for me."

48.

Statues of Liberty

THE FIRST TIME I REALIZED THERE WAS MORE THAN
one Statue of Liberty was several years ago, when I was reading
Umberto Eco's *Foucault's Pendulum*. The protagonist of this
densely plotted novel views the climactic scene from inside the
pedestal of a scale model of the Statue of Liberty, located—
along with the famous pendulum—in Paris' medieval abbey
church of Saint-Martin-des-Champs.

Intrigued, I made a point of visiting the former abbey
church on my next visit to Paris. But alas, the church—along
with the rest of the Musée des Arts et Métiers, which it
anchors—was closed for renovations. I checked up on their
progress whenever I was in the neighborhood, but at length
pushed it to the back of my mind.

And then, one afternoon while strolling in the Luxembourg Gardens, I remembered my quest. There, ahead of me,
was an unmistakable Statue of Liberty. It was smaller than

the original, of course, which would have towered over the treetops, but it was unquestionably a replica. How many times had I wandered through these gardens and never noticed her? She is located in the gardens' northwest corner, directly to the west of the octagonal pond.

This Lady Liberty is petite, less than ten feet high without her pedestal, and the tablet she holds has a November 1889 date. Deciding to look up her history, I discovered that she is one of five bronze replicas that the prestigious Thiébaut Frères foundry cast for several French cities following the 1886 dedication of the original in New York harbor. She is the only one of this group to have survived. The Germans melted down three for ammunition during World War II, while the fourth disappeared shortly after the war. The Luxembourg Gardens' statue survived. Thiébaut Frères cast her for her creator, Frédéric-Auguste Bartholdi, who gave her to the City of Paris for its centenary exhibition of 1900.

Bartholdi first had the idea of a gigantic statue following a memorable trip to Egypt. The Suez Canal was then nearing completion, and he proposed for its entrance a lighthouse consisting of an enormous female figure holding a lighted lamp. Bartholdi always protested that this Egyptian project (which never came to anything) had little influence on his Statue of Liberty.

Whether or not this was the case, when prominent French historian and politician Edouard de Laboulaye conceived of the idea of a huge monument to liberty as a gift from the French to the American people, Bartholdi enthusiastically signed on. The project clearly was in line with his passion to create a gigantic sculpture, on the scale of the ancient Colossus of Rhodes, but it also struck a chord with his deep commitment to the concept of liberty. Bartholdi fervently opposed the regime of Napoléon III as well as Germany's imperial outreach. Indeed, Bartholdi—who fought in the Franco-Prussian War—was devastated by France's defeat and the loss of his native Alsace.

Laboulaye seems to have been thinking in terms of sending an anti-Napoléonic message to the French as well as extending a remarkable gesture of friendship to America, and Bartholdi heartily approved. Liberty in France remained fragile, even after the Third Republic replaced Napoléon III, and republicans like Laboulaye and Bartholdi wanted to reinforce it with a powerful image. Completely committed to this cause, Bartholdi envisioned a gargantuan statue of Liberty Enlightening the World.

He nurtured his vision for many years, beginning with sketches and small study models (the Museum of the City of New York is the proud owner of one of these, dating from around 1870). Gradually, he progressed to larger models. The one in the Musée des Arts et Métiers is scaled at 1/16 the final version (about 9.5 feet, not including the pedestal). She stands on a dramatic rise at the far end of the church (originally the church entrance), standing on a pedestal shaped like a ship's prow. "Liberté, Egalité, Fraternité" is inscribed on the base. Within the hollow pedestal is a diorama that shows the completed Lady Liberty in New York Harbor.

The creation of this scale model marked the beginning of the actual fabrication of the final monument, which took place between 1875 and 1884. Bartholdi magnified this version to one that was four times as large (approximately 37 feet), and then divided this larger model into sections which he enlarged to their final dimensions (a whopping 151 feet, not including the massive pedestal).

The construction process itself was a remarkable undertaking, which the Musée des Arts et Métiers (60 Rue Réaumur, 3rd) rightly commemorates. Near its Lady Liberty are two tiny reproductions of the Paris foundry where Bartholdi wrought his final colossus. The one depicts his workmen in the process of enlarging a replica of Liberty's head, while the other illustrates the head's final assembly. The museum also has on display an impressive full-sized replica of Lady Liberty's index finger.

The foundry of Gaget, Gauthier et Compagnie (25 Rue de Chazelles, 17th), where Bartholdi constructed his gigantic monument, no longer exists, but it is well worth the trip to this attractive Parc Monceau neighborhood just to imagine the foundry's beehive of activity. The whole enterprise was so astonishing that Parisians paid to watch as the work progressed.

Bartholdi's partner in this daring undertaking was Gustave Eiffel, who engineered the statue's all-important substructure. Eiffel went on to build the tower that bears his name, but few today seem to realize his role in creating Lady Liberty. To do this, he devised a huge iron pylon that supported the statue's skin of shaped copper sheets. These he indirectly attached to the pylon by a skeletal framework of iron strips—a flexible construction that allowed the statue to withstand the changing temperatures and high winds of its future harbor home.

Gradually the statue began to rise—a startling vision above the housetops. After completion of her pedestal (an American effort, which took longer than expected), she made the long journey, in sections, to her final home.

The Statue of Liberty now graces New York harbor, where she remains a stirring symbol of the ideals for which both Americans and French have sacrificed so much, as well as of the bond of friendship that dates from America's earliest and most beleaguered days. Two additional Parisian replicas of the statue appropriately commemorate this bond. In the Place de l'Alma (8th/16th), there is a copy of the Statue of Liberty's torch, given by the *International Herald-Tribune*. This has become an informal memorial to Princess Diana, who met her death nearby. And on

Statue of Liberty, Ile des Cygnes

the southern tip of the Ile des Cygnes, beneath the Pont de Grenelle (15th/16th), rises a stunning replica of Lady Liberty, dramatically backed by Gustave Eiffel's tower.

This striking monument (a quarter-size copy, approximately thirty-seven feet high) was a gift to Paris from its American residents in commemoration of the French Revolution's centennial. A plaster version briefly stood in the Place des Etats-Unis (16th), but in 1889, French and American dignitaries dedicated the final bronze statue on the Pont de Grenelle. (The city moved her to the present location when the bridge was rebuilt.) Unlike the original Statue of Liberty, the tablet in this statue's hand commemorates both the French and the American Revolutions.

Throughout Paris there are many reminders of the long history of friendship between the two nations, but it is difficult to think of a more moving tribute than Lady Liberty herself. How fitting, then, that she should have sisters still residing in the city where she—and the impulse for this remarkable tribute—were born.

Founding Fathers

JOHN ADAMS, THOMAS JEFFERSON, AND BENJAMIN Franklin may not have always gotten along with one another, but they had at least two things in common: a deep devotion to their native land and—like so many Americans in the years to come—a love for Paris.

That Franklin and Jefferson delighted in Paris should come as no surprise. Their personalities and politics meshed well with the sophistication and liberalism they found here, at a time when Paris was daily growing closer to its own revolution. Jefferson received a warm welcome from Parisians eager to meet the author of the Declaration of Independence, while Franklin was treated as a hero—a man of science and a foremost figure of the Enlightenment.

But Adams—prickly, puritanical John Adams—seems an unlikely conquest. After all, Adams was as uncomfortable with court life as he was with revolutionary mobs, and held a firm conviction that the future lay across the Atlantic, in a newer and far more virtuous land. Unquestionably a hard case. And yet by the time he left Paris, Adams, too, had succumbed to Paris' beauty and culture. Always a walker, it can even be argued that he grew to know the city far better than either of his American colleagues.

Adams was the second of the trio to arrive, following Franklin, who had already established himself as a fixture in Parisian society. Franklin, who cultivated a homespun look, was anything but a country bumpkin. Although humbly born—the youngest son of a candle maker and soap boiler—he had quickly parlayed his considerable ability, hard work, and charm into a remarkable success story. Wealth gave him freedom to do what he wanted, which was to read widely, carry out his scientific experiments, and participate at ever-higher levels in the political affairs of the emerging American nation. This brought him to London, where for many years he represented the colony of Pennsylvania. By the time he arrived in Paris in late 1776, he had already lived a considerable portion of his adult life abroad.

Newly arrived in Paris, Franklin briefly stayed at 52 Rue Jacob (6th), on the Left Bank, where he enjoyed the company of other major thinkers and political activists at nearby Café Procope—a seventeenth-century establishment still very much in existence at 13 Rue de l'Ancienne-Comédie (6th). He then accepted the Comte de Chaumont's invitation to live at his estate in Passy. It was a shrewd choice from many standpoints, not the least being the fact that Chaumont—a wealthy merchant sympathetic to the American cause—provided his famous guest with every comfort. Surrounded by luxury and a bevy of servants, Franklin was free to continue his scientific experiments (he installed a lightning rod here) as well as carry out the business that brought him to Paris in the first place—that of securing French recognition and financial aid. Chaumont's estate lay on the western edge of Paris, conveniently near to Versailles and the seat of French power.

Chaumont's estate (formally known as the Hôtel de Valentinois) has disappeared, although the neighborhood remains an attractive one. The site of Franklin's comfortable dependency, on Rue Raynouard at Avenue du Colonel-Bonnet (16th), is marked with a large medallion and plaque. Rue Raynouard in turn leads directly to Rue Benjamin-Franklin and a fine statue of Franklin in the small Square Yorktown, just off the Place du Trocadéro. The other end of Rue Raynouard leads to 59 Rue d'Auteuil, where Franklin's dear friend, Madame Helvétius, lived and held her famous salon (the site is now occupied by a modern apartment building).

Lionized by Paris society and cosseted with every comfort—including the attention of numerous women, who seemed to find him irresistible—Franklin remained in Paris for eight years. Arriving two years after Franklin had established himself there, John Adams was dismayed by the splendor and casual amorality surrounding his colleague, not to mention Franklin's apparent indolence. That Franklin (one of three American commissioners sent to negotiate with the French) had already almost single-handedly persuaded France to recognize the new republic did not impress Adams. With his Puritan work ethic going full tilt, Adams seethed at Franklin's lack of energy in taking the next step—obtaining concrete French assistance in defeating the British in North America.

Taking lodging in the heart of Paris, at 17 Rue de Richelieu (1st), near the Palais Royal, Adams must have frequently passed the Hôtel Crillon on his many walks. Here, in February 1778, Franklin, along with Silas Deane and Arthur Lee, had signed that all-important treaty of friendship, commerce, and alliance with a representative of Louis XVI. The Hôtel Crillon, which with its sister palace flanks Rue Royale and forms the north side of the Place de la Concorde, was a favorite of Jefferson's and remains one of Paris' architectural glories. A marble plaque, almost hidden behind the pillars at the corner of Rue Royale, tells the treaty's story, but long before the plaque went up, Adams would have understood the building's consequence only too well. Arriving in Paris (to replace Silas Deane) only weeks after the treaty was signed, Adams felt that he had arrived too late.

His response was to work all the harder, making himself useful to the delegation and keeping up a voluminous correspondence. Chafing at French delays, he pressured the French foreign minister to act, only to be rebuffed. Soon after, Congress dissolved the commission and appointed Franklin as American minister to France. Adams returned home.

But this would not be Adams' last glimpse of Paris. Only weeks after returning to Massachusetts, Congress sent him back again, to negotiate peace with Great Britain once the fighting was over. Without missing a beat, Adams kissed long-suffering Abigail goodbye and sailed for France. This time, he brought with him his two eldest sons, John Quincy and Charles. (John Quincy, age twelve, had accompanied him on his first trip. Charles, age nine and reportedly a charming child, got to come along on this adventure. Parisians adored him.)

While still encountering professional frustrations, Adams continued his exploration of Paris, walking its gardens and streets—often in the company of his two sons. He introduced them to Left Bank bookshops and explored the gardens of the Tuileries and the Palais Royal. He took them to the Jardin du Roi (now the Jardin des Plantes, 5th), where they enjoyed poking about. Uneasy about the social and political structure that made such beauty possible, Adams nonetheless appreciated Paris' wealth of extraordinary architecture and sculpture, which also made a lasting impression on his eldest son.

After two years in Holland, during which Adams won Dutch recognition and a much-needed loan for the new nation, he returned to Paris for peace negotiations with Britain. These went on for some time, but at last, on September 3, 1783, Adams, Franklin, and John Jay signed the final peace treaty at the Hôtel d'York (56 Rue Jacob, 6th).

Adams briefly stayed at the Hôtel d'York with Abigail and daughter Nabby the following year, when they joined him and John Quincy in Paris (Charles had already returned home). They were all en route for Auteuil, where Adams had moved from his rooms in the center of Paris to far grander quarters, not far from Franklin's. This impressive mansion, boasting more than forty rooms, still remains at 45 Rue d'Auteuil (16th), although its acres of gardens have vanished.

Adams loved the peace and quiet of his new home, and he particularly enjoyed his walks in the nearby Bois de Boulogne. But Abigail was at first overwhelmed. She didn't know what to do with all those rooms and all those servants, especially since the rooms were barely furnished and the servants had a decidedly un-New England approach to work. Each considered himself a "specialist," unwilling to touch anything in another's domain. Worse yet, the ladies' maids even required their own hairdressers. Unhappily, this made a large staff necessary simply to scrape by.

Evidently Abigail had expected something quite different, for she had departed home bringing a cow with her (perhaps fortunately the cow died en route). But with typical aplomb, John Adams' remarkable wife quickly adjusted and took charge of her household. Mingling in Parisian society was more difficult, for her French was not nearly as fluent as her husband's (Adams had in fact worked considerably at it). Franklin's Madame Helvétius was not to her taste, but in time she came to admire the manners and intellect of certain Parisian women, especially the Marquise de Lafayette. In due course, this daughter of New England Puritans discovered that she enjoyed the theater and the opera, even if the women on stage were only scantily clad.

Thomas Jefferson must have smiled to watch her adapt and thrive in this dramatically different setting. He and his eleven-year-old daughter, Patsy, had arrived in Paris only shortly before Abigail and Nabby, and soon they all were fast friends. Jefferson, who was replacing John Jay in negotiating commercial treaties, fell immediately and irrevocably in love with Paris. The artist and the architect in him responded to the city's aesthetic, from its broad boulevards and public squares to its ever-growing number of fine buildings. In particular, he admired the fine new Place Louis XV (now the Place de la Concorde), so nobly situated on the banks of the Seine, between the Tuileries gardens and the broad sweep of the Champs-Elysées. As his eye appreciatively swept across the Place's broad expanses, it invariably came to rest on Jacques-Ange Gabriel's twin classical creations, flanking Rue Royale. These, in his view—and that of countless others—represented some of the finest architecture in Europe.

Jefferson had plenty of opportunity to gaze on the Gabriel buildings, for after initially taking Right Bank quarters on the cul-de-sac Taitbout, he moved to the Hôtel de Langeac (92 Avenue des Champs-Elysées, at the corner of Rue de Berri, 8th). This elegant mansion—still attractive, although nowadays somewhat spoiled by a ground-floor shop—was close enough to the Place de la Concorde that he regularly walked the distance, methodically counting the number of footsteps along the way.

Other fine buildings in the neighborhood that evoked his admiration were the Louvre's Grand Colonnade and the Hôtel de Salm (now the headquarters of the Legion of Honor, at 2 Rue de Bellechasse, 7th). Jefferson called both to the attention of Pierre L'Enfant in designing the new capital city of Washington, and if you look closely at the Hôtel de Salm from the river side, you can see the architectural forerunner of the White House.

Jefferson's social engagements as well as his daily walks regularly took him past the Hôtel de Salm, since the Marquis de

Washington and Lafayette, Place des Etats-Unis

Lafayette lived in a splendid house nearby. Lafayette, of course, had flung himself unhesitatingly into America's war for independence and, while in Paris, Jefferson frequently dined and discussed politics with him. A fine monument of Lafayette and George Washington, by Frédéric-Auguste Bartholdi, stands in the western end of the Place des Etats-Unis (16th), a lasting tribute to Franco-American friendship. Fittingly, an American flag always flies over Lafayette's grave in Picpus Cemetery (35 Rue de Picpus, 12th).

Within a year, Jefferson was appointed minister to France, while Adams left for the Court of St. James, and an ailing Franklin departed for home. Adams and Franklin, although maintaining an outwardly cordial relationship, could not have grieved much at the parting, but Adams and Jefferson were another matter. They had grown close during these months in Paris, and their friendship—despite some rocky years to come—would endure to the end of their very long lives.

Queen Marie Antoinette provided the comfortable litter that carried Franklin to his ship in Le Havre. But by the time Jefferson left Paris, four years later, the Bastille had fallen and a new order was dawning. Scarcely a decade after the American Declaration of Independence, the French were about to embark on their own momentous Revolution.

Neither Adams, Jefferson, nor Franklin returned to France. Franklin died in 1790, shortly after so memorably serving his country at its Constitutional Convention. Adams and Jefferson each became President in turn, then lived to see the fiftieth anniversary of the signing of the Declaration of Independence. And Franco-American friendship, after weathering some severe strains during the height of the French Revolution, continued.

Symbols of this long friendship can be found throughout Paris. In addition to all those evocative sites associated with our Founding Fathers, look for streets and Métro stops named for American places and Presidents, memorials dedicated to American statesmen (including a statue of George Washington in Place d'Iéna, 16th), and several small yet powerful versions of the Statue of Liberty (previously mentioned). Especially moving are two tributes to the ultimate sacrifice: a memorial in honor of the French who died at the Battle of Yorktown, 1781 (fittingly located by the Franklin statue in Square Yorktown, 16th), and Alfred Boucher's monument (in Place des Etats-

Unis, 16th) to those American volunteers who died for France in World War I.

Commemorating a more recent tragedy, an American oak is now growing in the Luxembourg Gardens, dedicated to the memory of the victims of September 11, 2001. This oak, planted to one side of the Luxembourg's Statue of Liberty, stands as a living and growing symbol of Franco-American friendship.

Two hundred years ago, three Americans ventured forth from their hearths and homes to cross the Atlantic and enter a society and culture vastly different from anything they had ever known. Rather than being rebuffed as provincials, they were welcomed as brave adventurers in a daring quest for liberty. Through the following years, countless Americans have followed, drawn by Paris' incomparable beauty, sophistication, and culture—and drawn as well by a link forged in friendship at our nation's outset.

They have not been disappointed. Like Abigail Adams, they have departed reluctantly. "Nobody ever leaves Paris but with a degree of *tristesse*," she confided. And she was right.

Index